L.C
42-16636
BD
431
.M885
12/19/1971

S0-AHE-367

The General
Theological Union
LIBRARY
Chicago, Ill.

WITHDRAWN

DEC 16 1976

Paths of Life

The Catholic

DEC 15 1976

Paths of Life

PREFACE
TO A WORLD RELIGION

Charles W. Morris

"This is my way. What is yours?
The *way there is none."*

NIETZSCHE:
Thus Spake Zarathustra

The Catholic
Theological Union
LIBRARY
Chicago, Ill.

THE UNIVERSITY OF CHICAGO PRESS
Chicago and London

The University of Chicago Press, Chicago 60637
The University of Chicago Press, Ltd., London

Copyright © 1942, 1956 by Charles Morris
Copyright © renewed 1970 by Charles Morris

All rights reserved. Published 1973

Printed in the United States of America
International Standard Book Number: 0–226–53879–6
Library of Congress Catalog Card Number: 72–94732

Contents

Preface

There is today, especially among young people, a widespread interest in what are variously called "ways to live," "life styles," "alternative value-patterns." This widespread interest is the reason for issuing this paperback version of *Paths of Life*, for *Paths of Life* is explicitly concerned with such matters.

It is felt that *Paths of Life* is more relevant to the contemporary situation than it was at the time of its publication in 1942. At that time, for most citizens of the United States, there was no problem of alternative ways to live—the superiority of the "American way of life" was largely unquestioned. But now that this country has encountered severe internal and international problems and frustrations, the exploration of a variety of possible ways to live has become an urgent task. And what is true of this country is true also of many other cultures.

Paths of Life is based on a discussion of six major life-orientations: the Buddhist, the Dionysian, the Christian, the Mohammedan, the Promethean, and the Apollonian. A seventh path of life, which I called Maitreyan, is proposed as a life-orientation peculiarly appropriate to contemporary man. I still believe this, and that it will appeal strongly to certain readers. But I wish also to stress the relevance of the book for those who aim to clarify their own commitment to whatever way to live they choose. All of the seven ways to live today have their advocates. It is believed that *Paths of Life* may clarify these living alternatives and their relations. This is the primary purpose of this edition.

This reprint is identical with the original version except that the 37 page section there called "Invocation" is here omitted. "Invocation' was essentially a poetic expression of what I meant by the Maitreyan path of life. For those interested in such a poetic expression I may refer to my two books, *Festival* (published in 1966 by George Braziller) and *Cycles* (published by The Tree of Life Press, Gainesville, Florida, in 1972).

For those interested in the scientific study of the materials in *Paths of Life,* I refer to my *Varieties of Human Values* (University of Chicago Press, 1956) and to an article written with Linwood Small, "Changes in Conceptions of the Good Life by American College Students from 1950 to 1970," *Journal of Personality and Social Psychology* 20 (1971): 254–60.

September 1972   CHARLES MORRIS

I. The Quest

"And he was withdrawn from them about a stone's cast, and kneeled down, and prayed,

"Saying, Father, if thou be willing, remove this cup from me: nevertheless not my will, but thine, be done.

"And there appeared an angel unto him from heaven, strengthening him.

"And being in an agony he prayed more earnestly: and his sweat was as it were great drops of blood falling down to the ground."

Luke 22:41-44

"Every man should follow his own religion. . . . As a mother, in nursing her sick children, gives rice and curry to one, and sago arrowroot to another and bread and butter to a third, so the Lord has laid out different paths for different men suitable to their natures. . . . People of this age care for the essence of everything. They will accept the essential of religion and not its non-essentials (that is, the rituals, ceremonials, dogmas and creeds)."

Sri Ramakrishna

"The great use of the gods is that they interpret the human heart to us, and help us, while we conceive them, to discover our inmost ambition and, while we emulate them, to pursue it."

George Santayana:
Reason in Religion

I

The Quest

THE agony of man is inherent in his life and inescapable. Man appears and lives in a world vaster and more powerful than himself; as a feeling and conscious being he is aware of this struggle to sustain himself, and aware of the relentless steps toward his own death. Ever struggling to reach his goals, achievements tempered by frustration and defeat; confused by the clash of his own assertiveness with the tug of detachment and the outreachings of sympathy and love; tolerated for a time by forces which support his strivings; invaded by processes which slowly break his delicate and precarious equilibrium; visited by intense joys and tragic pains, the thrust of life pushing him forward into the jaws of death: such is the human situation, the human agony. These are the vast and elemental features of man's life. This agony is inherent in human life and inescapable.

The ways in which men have met this agony vary with different individuals and with different times and places. To some persons the larger features of the process hardly rise to consciousness; to many there is available a formula which gives at least a specious unity and integration to their lives; some seek consciously and deliberately a controlling attitude to give to their lives coherence and direction. In one way or another, and with varying degrees of urgency, men have sought and still seek an attitude to life which will enable them to meet the human ordeal. This quest for an orientation of the total personality is the religious quest; those who point the way are the religious prophets ("the men of God"); the paths they have proposed are the foundations of the great religions.

It is with such paths of life, such ways of salvation, such techniques of orientation, such religions, that we are concerned. The terms 'salvation' and 'religion' must be understood in their widest sense: the most general mode for the conduct of life of an individual is that individual's way of salvation; the beliefs and techniques which underlie and implement that way constitute the religion of that individual.

There must be no confusion of salvation with any one particular set of religious terms such as 'God,' 'immortality of a spiritual soul,' 'heaven.' Indeed, the notion of religion has in the West become so associated with Christian supernaturalism that the wisdom of using expressions such as 'salvation' and 'religion' will immediately be called in question by many who might glance at these pages. These persons are at liberty to substitute whatever terms they prefer—such as 'total orientation' for 'salvation,' 'way of life' for 'religion.' Yet it does not seem advisable to bow too easily to the historical provincialism of Western culture: many contemporary students of religion have already begun to look at religious phenomena in terms of techniques for the orientation of life; and to abandon religious terminology to the advocates of a specific form of religion is to retreat before an issue that must be boldly faced.

That present-day man has reached a crisis in his cultural evolution is evident in countless ways. Disruption has broken out at all focal points. Poets, painters, novelists, political theorists, economists, psychopathologists, philosophers—all tell the same story of mingled despair and hope in different words and from different perspectives. The old cry—never far in the background —that "the end of the world is at hand" is again insistently in the foreground. Enormous wars, drastic economic changes, sharply contrasting political ideologies, rapid development in the sciences, emotional animosities in the clash of rival philosophies, basic revisions in educational systems, striking novelties in the arts, increase in the severity of personality disturbances, heightened indulgence in amusements, passion, drink as distractions—these are outward signs that the human agony has become acute. Prophets tell of a world that is falling and messiahs foretell a world that is to come.

All the focuses of individual and social disruption are active. Tentative gropings for new forms of personal relations jar the institutions in which such relations have been previously regulated; the allegiance to national groups struggles with allegiances to individuals, to classes, to mankind; an expanding technology which has increased the range of desires and the possibility of their satisfaction has simultaneously heightened the discontent of those to whom the new resources are not fully available; new forms of slavery and frustration confuse the belief that the individual by his own effort and the collaboration of the efforts of others could look forward to a progressively widening range of satisfied desire; the increase of scientific knowledge has modified traditional views of the cosmos and man's place in it; the thinking individual feels more strongly the antagonism of the modes of conduct indicated by his reflection, with the modes of conduct which are current about him; power laughs and love is confused, life has again been forced to look at death.

Such profound conflict inevitably produces a need for a basic orientation of the total personality. This is the religious need; and the evidence of the intensity of this need is everywhere at hand. There are deep stirrings in the old Orient; Europe is in turmoil; America stands hesitant before an uncertain future.

Old wisdom is being ransacked for guiding insights, and each of the dominant religious attitudes presents itself as a possible center of salvation. To explore the resources of the new religiosity, it is necessary to examine as deeply as possible the basic forms which the religious quest has assumed and may yet assume.

The paths posed and permitted by the human agony are few in number, though numerous in their elaborations and interpenetrations. After a preliminary account of human nature, six of the historic paths of life will be considered in turn: the Buddhist path of detachment from desire, the Dionysian path of abandonment to primitive impulses, the Promethean path of creative reconstruction, the Apollonian path of rational moderation, the Christian path of sympathetic love, the Mohammedan path of the holy war. We shall study the modes of life which these paths enjoin and something of the philosophies by which they are presented and defended. We shall see that each of them reflects a type of human personality. We shall find all of them active in the present crisis. In the analysis of these six paths, the outline of a seventh path—the path of generalized detachment-attachment—begins to be visible, and a new religion —Maitreyism—enters the struggle of religions to dominate the earth.

The attitude characteristic of the religion of Maitreya (the name of the future Enlightened One, the Friend, whose coming, according to legend, was predicted by Gautama Buddha) will be progressively developed through the discussion of the six paths of life which answer to the six types of personality so far dominant in human history; *Invocation,* at the end of the volume, attempts to suggest a religious expression of the attitude which the preceding pages approach through intellectual analysis. The hope and the conviction is that this attitude, as it clarifies itself and learns to speak boldly, may provide the germinal center for a world religion, and for a new epoch of human history: the Maitreyan epoch.

Our world is a babel of many voices. When a society is without a dominant and persuasive center of integration, the individual is forced back upon himself as a center. He must then make clear to himself what he is, what he would wish to be, of what form of society he would like to be a member. We are in such a period, as were the men of Hellenistic Greece. At such a time the term 'society' begins to lose its magic appeal; the individual and the differences between individuals come to the forefront of attention. It is out of the struggle between types of individuals that the new society is born. The form of this society will be determined by the types of individuals that come to dominance, and this in turn will be to some degree influenced by the reflection which individuals undergo. It is easy to make too much of the influence of individual intelligent choice, but it is even easier to make too little of it. For the selection of what attitude, what interest, is to be given dominance in the self, determines the range of activity permitted to every other interest in the self; let the Buddhistic preference for the desireless state really dominate a self, for instance, and specific attitudes to science, to philosophy, to war, to love, to art, to property, to society are more or less determined. Knowledge of physical nature and of man may aid—and should aid—in making such choices, but knowledge alone is not enough. Indeed, it is one of the ironies of this age that the very development of science —so essential to obtain the material upon which an intelligent choice can be built—has in many persons almost paralyzed the ability to make decisions; this irony has its counterpart in the fact that the preference for a scientific mode of statement has weakened the appeal of the religious, political, and moral symbols expressing the path of life through which science itself was given its justification and protection. Science is not itself an independent way of life; and it is unfortunate when it weakens the significance of those choices upon which even its own fate ultimately depends. In the last analysis the point of maximum leverage for the control by man of his destiny lies at the point where he raises the question as to what type of man he himself prefers to be and in whose hands he wishes to see the reins of social control. Such choices are the determinants of religion, and of the human future.

We shall study the dominant attitudes which men have assumed in the conduct of life. We shall attempt to be just and sympathetic, and we shall search in each one for utilizable wisdom. But the analysis is colored by a preference; it has an aim and a direction. We write the apologetics of Maitreyan man.

To whom then are these pages written?—baffling and disconcerting question an author dreads to raise. In a sense to everyone—so would every author like to believe even when in fact he writes only to himself, out of the urgency of his need to project himself before himself that he may release and enjoy his tensions in an outward vision. There is something here even for the problemless one, the irreligious one, who likes to savor casually, perhaps cynically, the diversity of human writhings in the trap of existence. But my concern has not been primarily with him. More to my heart have been those to whom life is

a problem, a task, an ordeal, something fascinating, challenging, intense, immense; those who demand some center of vision
that shall weave into a rope the strands of their multitudinous
life, tie it to the world-juggernaut, give it strength to follow
and to resist the tug of this great chariot. There are a number
of such ropes woven out of the diverse strands of diverse human
beings. We shall trace with friendly attention their patterns;
we shall even hope that these different types of persons gain
clarity as to themselves, and courage for the fate which their
characters have traced for them. And yet the warmth of our
heart is not impartial.

The image before my eye has been that of men and women
who "cannot go home again" to any of the religions, the philosophies, the forms of society which have yet been evolved.
Men and women using gratefully their biological and social
heritage, actively at grips with the processes of nature in which
life is lived, delighting in sharp thought and sharp perception.
Men and women who wish to bring together into a dynamic and
tensioned focus all the elements of human nature which the
traditional religions have indulged in isolation. Such individuals
will be equally sensitive to art, to science, to technology; they
are equally tired of self-indulgence, self-frustration, self-
obfuscation; they are equally bored with the waste lands and the
utopias which frustration has whined or sentimentalized. They
disdain the presentiment of doom under which courage is
paralyzed and the sentiment of inevitable victory under which
fear is narcotized. They wish to find a significant life in the
present, and to hide their heads neither in the sands of the
past nor of the future. They are tired of pretense, of hollow
formulas, of faked affection, of false security, of mechanical
activity. They have a sense for new horizons, the strength for
living through drastic social eruptions, the lightheartedness of

those who have relaxed the possessive grip on the self. Such individuals are among us, confused, lacking their appropriate symbols and instruments, often silent and withdrawn—but they are here, and in numbers. They deserve a justification of themselves, and a bold expression of their "religion," their "path of salvation," their "nirvana." I have written primarily for them.

II. Human Nature

"Mankind? It is an abstraction. There are, and always have been, and always will be, men and only men."

Goethe, to Luden

"The fact that all selves are constituted by or in terms of the social process and are individual reflections of it—or rather of the organized behavior pattern which it exhibits, and which they prehend in their respective structures— is not in the least incompatible with, or destructive of the fact that every individual self has its own peculiar individuality, its own unique pattern."

George H. Mead:
Mind, Self and Society

"Man's character is his fate."

Heraclitus

II
Human Nature

SINCE ways of life are actual or proposed forms of conduct for persons, we must begin our account by a consideration of human nature. We must be attentive both to the features which men have in common and which set the universal need for some dominant attitude of orientation, and to the features which distinguish men and account for the diversity of attitudes which have been utilized to meet the common need for orientation. And since each way of life, together with its supporting philosophy, is itself an expression of a particular type of personality, we cannot trust to any particular way of life for an account of human nature, but must turn to science for such a doctrine. The knowledge of man gained by science is still fragmentary and humble, but the developments of biology, the social sciences, and psychology bring us today at least to the threshold of an account of human nature which is rich enough to deal with the amazing complexity of men and women. And since our quest is not science as such, but a way of life, the larger features of the scientific attitude to man are alone relevant to our purpose.

In terms of present-day science it seems that man is one complex type of living being operating in a world of other things with which his destiny is inextricably linked; that he is best thought of as a dynamic and hierarchically organized system of interests or desires; and that conscious intelligence is, at least in degree, the characteristic which differentiates him from other

known forms of life. It is now necessary to make more explicit
these features which human beings have in common.

The embeddedness of man in, and his continuity with, other
processes of nature, has received overwhelming exemplification
in the reinforcement which science has given to common observations. It is obvious on every hand that the life of the individual is precariously dependent upon the world into which
he is born. Birth itself is an ordeal beset by countless hazards,
and the individual released from the womb is confronted with
endless difficulties in survival, and besieged with the constant
impact of objects fulfilling their own careers. Heat, air, water
—these must be present in amounts which need vary but slightly
for life to be impossible; great movements of the earth or of
heavenly bodies press alike upon fragile human flesh and fellow
living creatures; the flow of the rivers of society constrain within
narrow limits the flow of individual life.

More refined observations have made clear that the physical
and chemical processes which occur in man are part and parcel
of processes of much wider occurrence. The human body is a
complex system of living systems, delicate in its organization,
dependent for its existence upon the assimilation of other living
systems, invaded by similarly dependent systems of life. The
human mind is no exception: moods may fluctuate with the most
minute changes of the body and the environment; attitudes can
be transformed by changing the conditions under which life is
lived; thoughts vary with the exigencies which the living
system must meet.

That man is a complex and delicate balance of animate and
inanimate processes, poised in a network of similar processes

which at once provide the material for his support and measure the limit of his precarious existence: this is the net impression gained from common observation and reinforced by each advance of scientific knowledge.

Yet man is not simply clay on the potter's wheel of the universe: man is everywhere a valuer, an interested center of activity, a pursuer of goals. Physical and chemical processes have in living beings taken on the urgency of desire. Activities are not mere motions: they spring from needs and impulses which direct conduct in the search for objects to meet the motivating needs. Such directed conduct is an interest; its object is a value-object. The living being is a bent bow; its arrows are directed longings; its targets are its goals.

Human interests are amazingly diverse. It is true that the apparent diversity can be seemingly reduced: men have many interests in common and many activities can be regarded as variations upon a common interest which they share. It is the task of the scientist to make what order he can out of this diversity. Yet it is significant that diversity in the concrete remains, and no attempt to reduce all interests to forms of some common interest—such as the interest in happiness, or in power, or in love, or in survival—has met with common scientific agreement. It is of the nature of an interest to be a search for an object capable of meeting a need; nothing new is added by saying that the interest seeks satisfaction, or that men seek happiness or power. The search is for objects appropriate to specific needs; and interest may extend to all the complex things which make up the human and nonhuman world: to renunciation as well as to assertion, to pain as well as to pleasure, to death as well as to survival, to the attainment of knowledge as well as to the possession of objects, to concern for other persons and things as well as to concern for oneself. Some interests are more widespread than others and some are of greater strength, but an adequate doctrine of human nature must keep all in sight, and embrace all the characteristics which human beings display under all conditions. Man is in the end best characterized as a system of interests; the range and diversity of these interests distinguish him from all other living beings known to science.

The term 'system' is important here, but must not be pressed too far. A living being has many interests; but these are in dynamic interaction, and the fate of one has effects on the others; they vary in strength, and the open road which one interest has closes the road to others. What is true of the relation of the interests of an individual has an analogue in the interrelations of the interests of individuals in a society: there are social systems of interests constituted by the interrelations of individuals with each other. But the relation of interests within a system does not mean that all men have the same interests and in the same relations; or that the system of individual or social interests may not change its components or their relative strength; or that interests may not have relative degrees of independence from each other. To characterize man as a system of interests is to conceive him as a dynamically interacting set of specific interests.

Man is a system of interests—but a conscious system of interests. How is this factor of consciousness to be brought into the account? To say that man is a being with a mind is open to many ambiguities; it is better to say that man is a minded being. Yet even here caution is essential. In referring to mind we may merely call attention to the facts of feeling: to the pains, the joys, the sensed tensions which qualify the activities of a living being. All things have their qualitative aspects, and the felt qualities of the mutual impact of world and self (of the stimulation of delicate organs, of the satisfaction and frustration and shifting of interests) are incredibly variegated: they are the ways it feels to be alive.

But in referring to the mind we usually intend more than reference to the palette of feeling in which life paints itself: we refer to the processes of thought in which man extends the boundaries of his present world and lives in the light of things that have been, things distant from him, and things that may come in the future. Remarkable is this world of thought: its range is distinctive of man among the animals; it lifts the live being beyond the narrow limits of his immediate existence; it allows him to participate imaginatively in lives and processes which far outrun his own; it makes him the conscious witness of his own joy and agony; it has engendered the sciences and the arts and the religions; it has made of life and death insistent presences.

And yet if we follow the evidence, this mind of man is not a thing with a life of its own simply conjoined with the body: it is part of man's commerce with the world, born out of the aptitude of a living being to treat present things as signs of what is not present, an aptitude amplified and sustained by the fabric of communication with fellow men, and functioning in the service of the web of interests which constitute his life. It is a mode of his activity, a complicated tissue of sign processes, a quality which life has taken on; not a thing with a destiny independent of the vicissitudes of mortal existence.

It is true that science does not permit us to be dogmatic as to the finality of death: just as we cannot limit the universe to what we have encountered, so we cannot completely rule out the possibility that the processes which constitute an individual continue in some form or other beyond what we call his death. But if science prohibits dogmatism, the weight of its evidence speaks in favor of the finality of death, and of the conception of man as a complex being appearing in a wider universe, rising to consciousness and some degree of self-control, pursuing his interests by all the techniques of body and mind he can command, delicately responsive to features of the world which sustain or thwart his purposes, destined to disintegration in the larger world of which he is a concretion.

There is one feature of human nature so important that it must be brought into the focus of attention. Man is unique among living forms in the extent to which he has built social structures upon his physical and biological bases. Society, it is true, is not unique to man; animal societies are of enormous complexity. But man has evolved a distinctive type of cultural tissue in which is enmeshed nearly every feature of his activity, and it is a sea in which he does not always easily swim.

It is a common tendency of contemporary thought to stress the dependence of the most highly developed characteristics of the individual upon the social process in which he grows. The interests which he has, the types of activities in which he can engage, the tenor and direction of his thought processes, his very consciousness of himself: all these are in one way or another determined or effected by contact with the other members of the social group or groups of which a person is a member.

Of particular importance is the influence of the social matrix upon the interests which are grouped together in the term 'love.' In the widest sense of the term, anything that satisfies any interest is an object of love, and life, inseparable from interests, is inseparable from love. Anything may become an object of love, from the most transient object to the total cosmos. And in this wide sense of the term, love and death are the persistent features of life, inescapable for all men, influenced and molded by social structures but transcending any particular age or culture. Though the form of the religious life reflects inevitably the way in which a given society influences the interests of the members of the society and their possibilities of satisfaction, the quest for salvation has often been the search prompted by death for a stable object of love; and the universality of the quest has made it possible for particular religions to persist through diverse social changes. The process of living and dying is common to all men, even though the form of this process and the way and degree to which it is raised to awareness vary from group to group. In religion, as elsewhere, it is fatal to give priority to either the individual or society: some problems of the individual appear in any society, and no feature of the individual is free from the influence of the society in which he or she lives.

A narrower use of the term 'love' would confine love to an interest in the satisfaction of interests: to love someone is then to make the satisfaction of that person's interests one's active concern. In this sense of the term, there can be little dispute as to the existence of love, whatever may be its history and its range.

Love in this narrower usage is one interest among others, and can in principle be directed to any object which itself has interests. Morality will be regarded in this inquiry as love implemented by a concern for the fullest possible satisfaction of the interest of the loved objects; without an attempt to secure this satisfaction, love is passionate or compassionate or sentimental, but not moral. The area of morality may be narrow or wide: it may extend from a concern for one's own interest to concern for specific individuals, to members of a social group, to all men, and even to all living beings. Men differ in the range of their morality, their understanding of the interests of the persons they love, and in the effectiveness in which they help the satisfaction of these interests, but the difference is one of degree, and all men have to some extent a moral phase to their activity.

The most important segment of morality is social. Indeed so true is this that common usages would deny the ascription of the term 'moral' to active concern for one's own system of interests, or to the love of nonhuman animals, or even to persons outside of a given social class or group. When lives interact, the interests of the individuals mutually influence each other. Such a group in time develops approved ways of acting, so that the conduct of one individual is regulated in terms of the effect it has, or is thought to have, upon other individuals of the social group. These approved ways of acting are the group morality; the attempts of an individual to determine by reflection the action which gives the maximum satisfaction to a set of interests in conflict may in contrast be called reflective morality. Group morality and reflective morality may not coincide: approved modes of action may not be adequate to the actual interests of the group or may not be effective in realizing these interests; the actions of the reflective individual may likewise be inadequate or ineffective, or even if both adequate and effective, may be opposed to the actions approved by other members of the group. But in either case, the moral status of an action is determined by the relation of the action to a more comprehensive system of interests, and is in that sense social.

The results of envisaging naturalistically the development of the individual within the social group in which he is born have had profound implications in the conception of human nature. The full import of the genesis of the most distinctive features of the human self within the social group has been crystallized by George H. Mead in his volume, *Mind, Self and Society*. This approach turns inside out the ancient conception of the individual as endowed at birth with a "mind" through which he enters into social relations. It has traced the appearance of that mind within the processes of social interaction, and specifically within the process of linguistic communication. It has shown that man's ability to guide his conduct by reflection requires the operation of a kind of symbol made possible only within a social community. It argues that man's ability to consciously consider himself as an object arises only in a social process in which he at the same time becomes conscious of others. It traces the phenomena of conscience to the control which society exercises upon the individual in internalizing itself into the very structure of his personality.

Seen in this light, "man as man," man as "rational animal"

proves to be animal man as transformed by participation in social life. The individual is put back within society, and society itself within nature. The ancient dualism of body and mind (or soul) becomes transformed into the distinction of levels in which biologic man is complicated into social man. It no longer becomes possible to identify human nature with the particular modes of behavior characteristic of men in a particular society. The wholesale opposition of "individual" and "society" withers away at its roots, for what is characteristic of highly developed man turns out to require society for its nurture, while the highly developed societies require for their maintenance the very activities of such highly developed individuals which they have in turn made possible.

It was inevitable that Mead should even give the concept of salvation a social turn: the self, made possible by society, can envisage the outlines of a social order more congenial to its complex nature than the society in which it finds itself. The need for salvation, he writes in *The Philosophy of the Act*, is not the need for "the salvation of the individual but the salvation of the self as a social being. . . . The demand for salvation, where it swept over mankind as a whole, has gone along with the necessity of great social change." The religious need of the individual is itself generated out of the problems posed in him by participation in the society out of which he has emerged and which he no longer feels as adequate to his socially derived self.

We must, I believe, accept the results which such a social approach to the individual has obtained. We can no longer neglect in the study of individuals the social agencies by which diverse biological organisms have been given the common characteristics which they share as men and women—their minds, their morality, their consciousness of self. And yet if we stop there we have seen only one part of the story: we have neglected individual differences. To correct the emphasis it is necessary to focus our attention upon men and women as individuals.

The great interest in the social sciences in recent decades has drawn attention to the pervasive influence of a society upon its members; it has often obscured the differences between the members of a society and the effect of such individual differences upon the social structure. This one-sided emphasis, understandable historically, is now being corrected by the revival of an ancient interest in the nature of specific individuals and types of personality. This tendency is of especial importance for an investigation of the paths of life which men have followed, for the diversities of such paths are in some way correlated with the orientational problems of individuals, and the diversity of the answers is determined by the natures of various individuals, whatever may in turn be the conditions (physical, biological, and social) under which individuals with such natures have appeared.

A starting point is found in the view of man as a system of interests in which interests of greater strength control those of lesser strength. The controlling interest—if there be one—may be called the apical interest; it need not be assumed that there is any one apical interest common to all men (such as "happiness," "will to power") or that in any individual a particular apical interest is constant throughout his life. The question as to how far men at a given time, or throughout periods of time, have common interests, and how far these common interests have the same relative order of strength in different individuals, are matters for objective investigation. Such investigation, tentative though it yet is, would seem to favor the conclusion that there are a number of interests which all known men have in common (though the objects available to the satisfaction of these interests differ with various times and places), but that the relative strength of these interests differ in various individuals and are approved differently in various societies.

The existence of common interests may be elucidated by distinguishing three components of human personality: the *dionysian*, the *promethean*, the *buddhistic*. The dionysian component is made up of the tendencies to release and indulge existing desires in the presence of objects appropriate to the satisfaction of the desires. There is easy commerce of the individual with his world, and a reliance on that world, as it is, to satisfy the desires as they are. There is hunger, and one eats what will satisfy the hunger; there is sexual desire and one has sexual intercourse; there is a desire for companionship, and one seeks the company of friends. The self sinks itself in the available world and that world supports the demands of the self.

But this gracious interplay of self and world is seldom attained. Man is active even in the satisfaction of desires; for the most part he must in addition act in order to find and make secure the objects which will satisfy his interests. The promethean component of personality is the sum of these active tendencies to manipulate and remake the world in the service of the satisfaction of existing desires.

The world, physical and social, is, however, often recalcitrant. Desires may not be fully satisfied, or may be denied any satisfaction whatsoever. The wariness which is already involved in promethean activity (since desires are held in abeyance until manipulation finds or makes the appropriate objects) is transferred to the desires themselves. The buddhistic component of personality comprises those tendencies in the self to regulate itself by holding in check its desires. These are the tendencies to self-control, to solitude, to meditation, to detachment, to self-containment.

Man has at his disposal three corresponding emphases in the conduct of his life. He may merely "let himself go," relying on and utilizing the world as it presents itself; he may attempt to modify the world in which he lives so that his desires are more adequately realized; he may so modify or restrain his desires that the frustrations imposed by the world are avoided or minimized. Indulgence of his existing desires, control of the environing world, control of himself: these are the tactics open to a being whose life is commingled with the press and pull of vaster processes.

Where three weapons are available, it is not wisdom to rely on one alone, and harassed man has made the best use of the tactics of releasing, remaking, and restraining which his own nature and the conditions under which he operates permit. He has simply satisfied his desires when the objects of satisfaction were at hand; otherwise, attempts to control a stubborn world are persisted in as long as possible; the expedient of disciplining desires commends itself only when serious obstacles present themselves to the satisfaction of desire. And even when this expediency arises it may be quickly forsaken when the surrounding world presents a more inviting view. So compromise and alternation of tactics is the rule: some desires are denied expression and some are held in check until a favorable environment has been constructed; some are allowed immediate satisfaction; and a desire reined in at one moment will be given freedom at a later moment.

Different individuals are dionysian, promethean, buddhistic to different degrees. Such differences are not unique to man, and the fact that animals show marked divergences in the extent to which they are easygoing, energetic, cautious, suggests that the differences are grounded in fundamental biological structures.

The distinction of the dionysian, promethean, and buddhistic components of personality, and the attempt to explain the different types of personality in terms of the different combinations of these components, was originally suggested through the study of the major types of religion; the search was for a method of understanding what lay behind, and was expressed in, the different paths of life proposed by, say, the Buddha, Christ, Aristotle, Nietzsche, Dewey. The theory of personality which resulted was accordingly based on material drawn from one phase—a primarily literary phase—of human culture, and its adequacy for the problem which generated it is to be decided in terms of such analysis as the following chapters present; it is not necessary to rest these analyses upon any particular scientific theory as to the ultimate sources of individual differences.

However, in the course of this study, contact was made with the work of W. H. Sheldon, and his biologically grounded theory of personality served both to confirm the initial direction of analysis and to sharpen its initial vagueness. Sheldon regards the temperament of the individual as a function of three sets of traits which he calls, respectively, viscerotonia, somatotonia, and cerebrotonia. The study (*Physique and Temperament*) which is to contain the developed theory has not yet appeared, but these traits are given a preliminary description in his volume *The Varieties of Human Physique*:

> The extreme *viscerotonic* temperament is characterized, among other things, by a general relaxation of the body as a whole. The viscerotonic is a "comfortable" person. He loves comfort:

soft furniture, a soft bed, luxurious surroundings. He also radiates comfort. He participates easily in social gatherings and makes people feel at home. He exhibits an extraversion of affect by showing a warm interest in many people and a genuine tolerance of their personalities. Whatever his feelings he expresses them easily. His joys and sorrows he communicates to others. Food is of great importance in the life of the viscerotonic and his fondness for fine food and ceremonious eating is backed by a good digestion and an ability to dispose of large quantities of "roughage."

In the extreme *somatotonic* we encounter an active, energetic person—a person addicted to exercise and relatively immune to fatigue. He walks assertively, talks noisily, behaves aggressively. He stands and sits with an upright posture and in youth presents the general appearance of a maturity beyond his years. He is concerned mostly with affairs of the present and meets his problems with some form of activity. His is an extraversion of action rather than of affect.

The extreme *cerebrotonic* is an "introvert." He is under strong inhibitory control as regards expression of feeling—he is unable to "let go." His history usually reveals a series of functional complaints: allergies, skin troubles, chronic fatigue, insomnia. He is sensitive to noise and distractions. He is not at home in social gatherings and he shrinks from crowds. He meets his troubles by seeking solitude.

In another passage he summarizes these characteristics and connects them more specifically with biological categories:

Viscerotonia is roughly identifiable with love of comfort, relaxation, sociability, conviviality, and sometimes with gluttony. It is the motivational organization dominated by the gut and by the function of anabolism. Somatotonia is the motivational pattern dominated by the will to exertion, exercise and vigorous self-expression. It is the drive toward dominance of the functions of the *soma*. Cerebrotonia refers to the attentional and inhibitory aspect of temperament. In the economy of the cerebrotonic individual the sensory and central nervous systems appear to play dominant roles. He is tense, hyperattentional and under strong inhibitory control. His tendency is toward symbolic expression rather than direct action.

It is suggested that there is a close connection between temperament and physique, so that the highly cerebrotonic temperament is physically strongly ectomorphic (dominated by the structures of the brain and eye developed from the ectodermic layer of the embryo), the highly somatotonic temperament is physically strongly mesomorphic (dominated by the striped musculature developed from the mesodermic layer of the embryo), and the highly viscerotonic temperament is physically strongly endomorphic (dominated by the visceral organs developed from the endodermic layer of the embryo). In so far as such a correlation holds, it would seem as if the differences of personality lay biologically in the order of dominance of the visceral, striped-muscular, and cerebral systems of the individual organism. In so far as the correlation does not hold, one would suspect that an explanation must be sought in terms of the character of the physical and social context in which the biological organism grows: a personality presumably is the result of the interplay of a specific biological organism and a specific physical-social environment.

Correlations must be used with caution; nevertheless it seems that Sheldon's position dovetails in the main with the results independently obtained in attempting to understand the personalities which lie behind the various paths proposed for the conduct of life: 'dionysiac' correlates to some extent with Sheldon's use of 'viscerotonic,' 'promethean' is perhaps trans-

latable by 'somatotonic,' and 'buddhistic' by 'cerebrotonic.'
While we shall continue to use the original and more expressive set of terms, Sheldon's terminology and description serves
to amplify and concretize the traits of personality to which attention is here called. The exact relation between his and the
present approach can be discussed only when Sheldon's results
have received their detailed presentation.

We shall regard an individual person as characterized by
a particular order of strength of dionysian, promethean, and
buddhistic traits. Thus in one individual the buddhistic component may be dominant over the promethean and that in turn
over the dionysian; such an individual would tend to alert
self-control and detachment, would however be active and
energetic, and would resist a life of sensuous comfort. There
is, theoretically, a continuum of individuals differing in these
respects; but, practically, it is possible to classify individuals
through the degree to which the factors of personality have
the same relative strength and order. And from this procedure
arises the notion of a type of personality.

The number of types of personality distinguished is relative
to the degree of similarity in order and strength of the components chosen as the basis of classification. For present purposes a relatively small number of types is sufficient. If we
consider only the order of strengths of the dionysian, promethean, and buddhistic traits, and do not attempt to discrim-
inate the strengths within a given order, we obtain a classification of human personalities into seven major types, to which
we assign specific names:

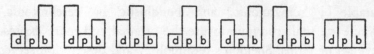

Buddhist Dionysian Promethean Apollonian Christian Mohammedan Maitreyan

A number of comments are relevant. There may be some danger of confusion in using the same stem to designate both a component of all personalities and a specific type of personality, thus: 'dionysian' and 'Dionysian.' On the printed page, the use of small and capital letters marks the distinction; if confusion is likely, especially in speaking, it may be advisable to shift to another set of terms (or to the initial letters of the terms here used) to label the components of personality.

There is no magic virtue in the number seven; this number merely results from the method of classification employed. For other purposes, or even for a refinement of the present type of analysis, further distinctions may well prove to be convenient. Nevertheless, since the present seven types are exhaustive of the logical possibilities involved in using three basic sets of character traits (provided a convention is made to determine the classification of individuals in whom two components are of the same strength), any such further distinctions can be made within the seven types here outlined, as subtypes of Buddhists, Prometheans, or what not. The present procedure, while coarse, is nonetheless all-inclusive.

The distinctive feature of personality does not lie in the bare predominance of one component, but in its predominance in relation to the other components. Thus the Christian and Buddhist are both predominantly buddhistic (cerebrotonic), but there are marked differences in their personality: the relatively high dionysian component of the former will suffuse his detachment with a sublimated affective warmth (Christian contemplation becomes an intellectualized love of God, always near to mysticism), while the low promethean component will give to this personality a certain passivity (dependence on God's grace, upon the Church); the Buddhist in contrast, being less dionysian and more promethean, is more narrowly intellectualistic, his love is more kindly and less mystic, and he tends to take the control of himself into his own hands.

This example also makes clear that we cannot simply correlate one kind of attitude ("sociality," "rationality") with the dominance of a particular component. It is true that in general the highly buddhistic individual is inclined to abstract reasoning and to solitude in a way foreign to the highly dionysian individual, but such generality is misleading: the highly buddhistic Christian is sufficiently dionysian to seek a society in which his love can express itself, and yet sufficiently detached to be uncomfortable in the rough and ready society ("the world") in which less buddhistic individuals find themselves congenitally at home; the detachment of the Buddhist may not take the form of highly intellectualized "scientific" reasoning in a society in which such intellectuality is insufficiently developed or deliberately repressed. It must be kept in mind that the mode of expression of any one component of personality is influenced by the strength of the other components as these operate in a particular physical and social environment.

It is our conviction that the major types of personality express themselves in different philosophies, forms of art, types of society, varieties of religion. Even the features of conduct they have in common with other individuals of different types will bear their own unique imprint: the way they use symbols, the attitude to morality, the manifestation of love, the orientation of their intellectual life, the forms of insanity, the evaluation of whatever is evaluated. Some references to these differences will come into the account, but attention will center upon the general attitudes by which persons of various types have expressed themselves and given direction to their lives. We envisage the religious quest as the quest by the individual for a way of life answering to his type of personality, whether that be the type he has already attained or the type which seems to point a way out for the conflicts of his as yet unsettled and uncertain self.

It lies in the very nature of an interest or interest system to seek objects appropriate for its satisfaction and to struggle with thing, animal, or person that prevents access to these objects; within the interest system of an individual there is competition between the component interests for dominance at a particular time, and a constant shift in the relative strength of interests at various times; between individuals there is the friction imposed by the simultaneous existence of diverse types of personality; the rivalry between social groups (whether classes, nations or groups of nations) exhibits on a large scale the conflict between the types of personality whose dominant or preferred status characterizes the diverse social groups in question. Struggle, conflict, frustration, aggression are inherent in the tissue of interlocking interests which constitute individuals and societies; they may be ordered and regulated as the component interests and interest systems are ordered, but they cannot be abolished.

Whether seen from the focus of the individual or the focus of the social group the picture is the same. The personality of the individual is influenced both by the biological characteristics of the individual in question and by the type of person-

ality favored by the social group to which he or she belongs.
Suppose that an individual is physically inclined (though not
without struggle) to dominance of the buddhistic component,
but lives in a society in which personalities strong in the promethean component have a preferred status. The conflict between the various traits within the individual is then complicated by, and must be resolved in the face of, the social system
in which he lives. His conflict is both individually and socially
conditioned, engendered by the competition of the components
of his own personality and his contact with other types of personality. This conflict may not in some individuals be severe:
the relative strength of some component of the personality may
be so great that it controls without much difficulty the other
components, and the environing social group may favor and
facilitate this control. But in the case in question, the control
by the buddhistic component, made difficult by the relatively
high strength of the other components, is intensified by the
group opposition to the path of life to which the individual
tends. It is in such situations that the personality disturbances
studied by the psychopathologist come most sharply to the forefront, and it is clarifying to see these conflicts in terms of a
struggle conditioned both by the relative strength of the three
components of personality in the individual and by the contacts
of this individual with persons of the same or different types
of personality. Particular types of individuals are prone to particular conflicts (as they are to certain diseases of the body),
but the severity of the conflict and the measures adopted to
meet it will be influenced by the pattern of the society of which
the individual is a member. Thus the "buddhistic" individual
in question may attempt to assume the approved promethean
characteristics, but they do not ring true, and though he gets
social approval for his attempt, he may not be able to compete

effectively with those to whom the type is more congenial, while his assumed role will in any case clash with the suppressed buddhistic tendencies of his nature; or the individual may attempt to remain true to his buddhistic impulses by retiring as far as possible from the promethean society—and thereby incur the disapproval of that society. And so on with variations due to differences of various individuals immersed in various societies. The path that an individual endeavors to follow may not be the path most congenial to his nature, but may represent a forced attempt to control his stronger impulses by the other components of personality, whether or not these are approved by the society of which he is a member. It is in such terms that the problems of psychopathology are to be posed.

Viewed from society as a focus, the situation is similar. Since social groups are composed of individuals, the pattern of a society can only be the pattern of the types of personality of its members: the society will be characterized by the order of dominance of certain types of personality and the struggle of more dominant types with the less dominant ones. There are some groups markedly dionysian in character; in Western civilization the reins have been in the hands of those strongest in promethean characteristics; in certain parts of the Far East buddhistic characteristics have been favored. In any such group, individuals of other types will have to adjust themselves as well as they can, either by attempting to conform to the approved path of life, or by endeavoring to change the society, or by going their own way in spite of whatever social opposition they may call forth. These conflicts within the society may go so far that the society loses an effective form of organization, and becomes the interplay of struggling social groups each attempting to give to the society the characteristics of the type of personality which they particularly favor. At such times we witness the struggle of a society to attain a path of life that can orient or integrate the society as a whole, and the struggle by individuals to attain a path of life which will at least offer them salvation and perhaps serve as a basis for a new social order.

Such is the present situation of man. It marks the ordeal of present culture and defines the present form of individual agony. All the paths of life which formerly integrated the lives of individuals and societies struggle in our midst for our individual allegiance, and for earth-dominance. The account of human nature will become richer and our understanding of the contemporary crisis deeper if we survey in turn each of these paths. We can then return more wisely to the problem which the present makes insistent: the adopting of an attitude to control the conduct of our own lives and direct if possible the future course of human evolution. Large issues are at stake. The ordeal of men and of mankind has become acute.

III. The Buddhist Path of Detachment from Desire

"Thus, monks, as I reflected, my mind turned to inaction, not to teaching the Doctrine. Then Brahmā Sahampati knowing the deliberation of my mind thought, 'verily the world is being destroyed, verily the world is going to destruction, in that the mind of the Tathāgata, the arahat, the fully enlightened, turns to inaction and not to teaching the Doctrine.' Then Brahmā Sahampati, just as a strong man might stretch out his bent arm, or bend his stretched-out arm, so did he disappear from the Brahma-world and appear before me. And arranging his upper robe on one shoulder he bent down his clasped hands to me and said, 'may the reverend Lord teach the Doctrine, may the Sugata teach the Doctrine. There are beings of little impurity that are falling away through not hearing the Doctrine.' Thus said Brahmā Sahampati."

Majjhima-Nikaya

III

The Buddhist Path of Detachment
from Desire

THE picture of man which has been sketched, though it could be amplified in numerous details and supported at will by the testimony of men of letters and men of science, will undoubtedly appear grim in some eyes, and would be as offensive to many men of past ages as it is to many persons today. And yet hardly anything in this picture would have surprised the early adherents of Buddhism some twenty-five hundred years ago. The terminology would often have seemed strange to them, but not the content. They saw the life of the individual embedded in the wider play of cosmic forces; they recognized that the human dilemma was posed by the clash of insurgent desire with a world which offered opposition and frustration; they analyzed the individual into a complex of factors which had come together and which must eventually suffer dissolution; they recognized that the religious life was the quest of the individual for salvation in his human ordeal; they were clear that the urgency of this need and the question of its possible solution was independent of whether the individual was or was not immortal; they taught that the individual by his own conscious recognition of his position in the world and by his own activities must attain salvation for himself. Gautama Buddha was merely the discoverer of the path, a man who had attained salvation (nirvana) in this life by his own insights and activities; he could indicate the path, but each must traverse it alone.

Gods were not denied, to be sure, but the gods were not thought of as the creators or directors of the world; they were themselves beings caught up in the great process, not saviors of men but beings themselves in need of salvation; the Buddha, the Enlightened One, was equally the teacher of men and gods. The words attributed to him as his last words were for the ears of all that live: "Decay is inherent in all component things; work out your salvation with diligence." Buddhism was to supply the technique by which salvation could be attained in a world in which all component things suffered dissolution.

The path of salvation which the Buddha indicated is often characterized as the path of detachment from desire. The grand simplicity of the basic conceptions and the detailed delineation of their consequences make of Buddhism one of the masterful achievements of human culture.

The central conceptions spring from regarding desire as the basic factor of life, and the existence and frustration of desire as the basic sources of human suffering. The remedy of the Great Physician is based on the diagnosis: desire is the arrow in the side of suffering life; remove the arrow and the wound will heal. Recognize that the source of suffering lies in attachment; progressively extinguish the flame of desire; and there will in time come the cool peace of detachment, of nirvana, of freedom from desire.

The attainment of the attitude of detachment was a long and arduous one. The enemies were numerous:

> Be advised that sensual desires are the 1st Army of thine enemy; that discouragement and sadness are the 2nd Army; that hunger and thirst are the 3rd Army; that attachments are the 4th Army; that laziness and sleepiness are the 5th Army; that fear and fright are the 6th Army; that doubt and remorse

are the 7th Army; that hatred is the 8th Army; that selfish love of comfort and praise are the 9th Army; that egoistic pride and complacency are the 10th Army. All of these armies of evil beset the follower of Buddha.

Desire was seen to be inherent in living beings, and no short cut would remove it. Slothful indifference by some version of the doctrine that death was itself annihilation was not permitted: the fate of the individual after death (and after the attainment of nirvana) was held to be undetermined, and suicide was repudiated as a means of deliverance. Nor were the extremes of asceticism tolerated: the Buddha himself had practiced austerities unto emaciation, and had rejected such excesses; he had perhaps realized that there is hidden under the extremes of self-castigation a fanaticism incompatible with the attitude of detachment.

The path outlined was pictured as a middle way between the extremes of mortification and indulgence. The individual was to simplify his existence by giving up the family mode of life, by refraining from sexual relations, by owning nothing but his robes, his cot, and his alms bowl. This existence involved a radical but not absolute withdrawal from the common social life. The individual associated with others with the same goal, and he shared with whoever would listen the fruits of his own development; he did not condemn society at large or set about to transform it; he did not expect a future period of society in which human ills would be absent; he went his own way to salvation and he would show the way to those who wished to follow it. His own life was spent in obtaining enlightened self-control. Morality was not repudiated, but was regarded as only part of the path of controlling the turbulence of desires, and not the goal. The heart of the religious life was found in the search for emancipation from ignorance and ultimately from desire.

The purpose of the Holy Life does not consist in acquiring alms, honour, or fame, nor in gaining morality, concentration, or the eye of knowledge. That unshakable deliverance of the heart: that, verily, is the object of the Holy Life, that is the essence, that is its goal.

Solitude was essential so that the individual might meditate upon himself and come to know his own nature, and to become strong in himself as his own center. In this meditation he did not permit himself indolence or the loose play of thoughts and emotions. Aspect by aspect of himself was raised to consciousness, its nature known, its connection with desire and suffering seen; doubt, distraction, the longing for fame, aversion, lust, hypocrisy, cowardice, malice, pride, ignorance, reliance on mere ritual, belief in a permanent individuality, desire for existence, desire for nonexistence, were to be rooted out; the whole being was to become alert, concentrated, focused, desireless, imperturbable, impregnable. Nirvana would come with the extinction of craving for existence and nonexistence alike; nirvana itself would not even then be craved; detachment would be complete.

As I thus knew and thus perceived, my mind was emancipated from the āsava of sensual desire, from the āsava of desire for existence, and from the asava of ignorance. And in me emancipated arose the knowledge of my emancipation. I realized that destroyed is rebirth, the religious life has been led, done is what was to be done, there is nought (for me) beyond this world. This was the third knowledge that I gained in the last watch of the night. Ignorance was dispelled . . . light arose. So is it with him who abides vigilant, strenuous, and resolute.

The traits of character which the Buddhist condemns are those that involve a person in the world; he approves of those traits which aid the self's self-conquest, subdue its tendencies to indulgence and assertion, detach it from all involvement:

> Whoso have no one thing beloved, they have no sorrow.
> Sorrowless are they and passionless. Serene are they I declare.
> Make thou in all the world nought dear to thee.

Before attempting to assess the path of detachment from desire, let us amplify our understanding of the doctrine by what may seem at first to be a digression. In the history of Buddhist thought the question as to the status of nirvana was a center of controversy. Did an emancipated one continue eternally in the state of nirvana or was nirvana merely a state occurring at a certain period of time in the life of the individual? The problem involves the whole relation of salvation to duration. Its consideration was complicated by the Buddhist's acceptance, simultaneously, of a doctrine of transmigration, a doctrine of "non-soul," and the relegation to the status of an undetermined question the problem of whether one who has attained enlightenment exists or does not exist after death.

The literature of early Buddhism makes clear that salvation was something that could be attained by the individual in his own lifetime; the Buddha attained nirvana in middle life, and lived until eighty. Nirvana would seem to have been envisaged as a state of life, the fruit of having attained the attitude of detachment from desire; and the question of its duration in time was irrelevant. The "undetermined questions" of philosophers (including the existence or nonexistence of the saved ones) were specifically dismissed as being irrelevant to the religious quest: they did "not tend to advantage of the religious life, to aversion, absence of passion, cessation, calm, insight, enlightenment, Nirvana." The religious life, accordingly, was something which could be lived within the limits of human life; salvation required no doctrine of the immortality of the individual or his entrance into some supernatural "other world."

This attitude to salvation is only apparently contradicted by the Buddhist acceptance of the then current doctrine of transmigration. For this doctrine was interpreted in a way which did not involve the doctrine of a spiritual substance which successively entered into various bodily forms. It is true that the doctrine of the annihilation of the individual at death, found among some Buddhists, was rejected officially as a dogma; but equally clear is the rejection of the self as an immaterial self-identical substance passing from existence to existence. The Buddhist psychology analyzes the individual into a compound of a number of factors; this aggregate may indeed persist with various modifications beyond what is humanly described as its death—and the history of these persistences and the causal effects of the individual's action (and not the history of an identical soul substance) constitute the history of transmigration. But this reservation does not mean that the career of the individual runs throughout all time: indeed, the attainment of nirvana is presented as the cessation of desire and the consequent extinction of rebirth. It is not at all clear whether in the light of these factors it is even intelligible to ask whether the state of nirvana exists or does not exist after the wheel of transmigration has been stopped; and in any case the Buddhist's refusal to answer the question (if question it be) is consistent with his general attitude of detachment from desire: the goal is the attainment of a state of life; to desire that this state continue to exist or not continue to exist is to remain within the web of desire.

Early Buddhism offers a position of great significance to those engaged in the religious quest. It presents a path of life and a view of salvation conceived within the limits of human existence, not dependent upon any splitting of the universe into the natural and the supernatural, and not dependent upon any doctrine of the immortality of gods or men.

Buddhism in its essentials is a religion independent of any special system of metaphysics and favorable in principle to any increase of scientific knowledge concerning man or the cosmos. Nevertheless, Buddhism did in the course of time develop a philosophy, and the question can be raised as to how far this philosophy is required by, or helpful to, the Buddhist techniques for salvation.

For approximately five hundred years Buddhism remained a way of life relatively free from the consideration of philosophical issues. But in the second five hundred years, in the *Mahayana* development, Buddhism became a philosophy of the idealistic type more and more akin to the metaphysical systems which the Buddha had put to one side as indifferent for, if not hostile to, the religious life. Into this development itself we will not go in detail; it is sufficient to say that the early common-sense naturalistic view of man inhabiting a wider universe was increasingly questioned, and was gradually replaced by a view that "mind" or "consciousness" alone was "real." The apparent natural world became a world of appearances only, comparable to a magician's show, and Buddhist thought found itself on the edge of those systems of metaphysics which center around an unknowable Absolute and its appearances. This is not our domain; but since we are tracing the major human attitudes, it is worthy to note the seductive tendency of those who seek salvation by the control of the self to deny as "unreal" the world which initially posed their very problem of salvation. However, the price paid is high, for while it seems an aid to the solution of the problem of life to deny the existence of a world which blocks desires, the existence of the desiring individual himself becomes questionable in this process, and the solution as imaginary as the problem: the attainment of nirvana is itself finally regarded as only part of the illusory surface show:

> The Buddha does not attain Nirvana;
> The Doctrine does not pass away;
> But for the sake of ripening beings
> He makes a show to attain Nirvana.

It would be dogmatic to dismiss as philosophy these views of later Buddhism; it is not dogmatic to say, in the spirit of early Buddhism, that the question of their truth and falsity "does not tend to the advantage of the religious life. . . . There is still birth, there is old age, there is death, grief, lamentation, suffering, sorrow, and despair, of which I preach the destruction even in this present life."

The history of Buddhism makes insistent, however, the question as to the wisdom of the early Buddhist's attempt to put to one side, as irrelevant to the religious life, the systematic construction of a philosophy. It was the vagueness of the relation of nirvana to temporal processes, and vagueness as to the ultimate destiny of the self, which introduced into later thought the temptation to transform nirvana into a nonnatural mode of existence which would be enjoyed "eternally" by the self which

had put off the fetters of mortality. Unless an explicit theory
of mind and selfhood is given, and the common-sense naturalism of the early position is made explicit and defended, the
temptation is strong for the Buddhist attitude to develop into
an idealistic philosophy in which the very urgency and relevancy
of this attitude is sapped by a view of the world in which
the generating problem which directed the religious quest is denied to be a real problem at all. A revived Buddhism should
profit by the history of Buddhism, and align itself deliberately
with the scientific attitude and the empirical and naturalistic
cosmology which such an attitude involves.

Parallel to the invasion of Buddhistic thought by metaphysics,
there was an increasing resort to mythology and to magical and
emotional supplementations of the path to salvation.

Gautama Buddha, having attained enlightenment, was
tempted to remain undisturbed in that state. We have seen that
morality and love, of which morality is a form, played only
a subordinate role in early Buddhism as stages on the path of
individual salvation (indeed, it seems not unfair to say that the
Buddhist used the control of man's animal nature, which the
common morality sanctions, as a means to his own struggle for
self-sufficiency and ultimate self-surrender). So the temptation
of the Buddha to keep to himself the fruits of his labor is
natural enough. But now an interesting development occurs,
prefigured in the Buddha's determination to preach the doctrine
to others out of compassion for all living things. The bodhisattva
ideal arises: the ideal that those destined to Buddhahood should
follow a long and arduous career through many reincarnations
because of love for others, renouncing nirvana for themselves

until it is attained by all sentient creatures. There even appears the doctrine that "for Buddhas there is no Nirvana."

In the perfect self-realisation of Noble Wisdom that follows the inconceivable transformation death of the Bodhisattva's individualised will-control, he no longer lives unto himself, but the life that he lives thereafter is the Tathagata's universalised life as manifested in its transformations. In this perfect self-realisation of Noble Wisdom the Bodhisattva realises that for Buddhas there is no Nirvana.

This coming to the foreground of the principle of love, in a form so strong as to postpone indefinitely the individual's attainment of salvation, is of profound significance; for love is a form of attachment to the development of others (just as concern for one's own salvation is a form of self-love), and to accept a long course of suffering in the service of this love is for all practical purposes to remain indefinitely attached to life, to struggle, and to suffering, as well as to others. Later, in a consideration of Christianity, it will be necessary to probe the impact of love upon the religious life; in the present connection it is only necessary to point out the concessions made by the principle of detachment from desire, involved in the heightened importance of compassionate love in later Buddhism. The mythological picture of countless Bodhisattvas and Buddhas, laboring and suffering through many births to aid the salvation of all living beings, involved no theoretical repudiation of the goal of detachment (indeed to some degree it evidenced the application of detachment to nirvana itself), but in practice it unquestionably indicated the power of the forces which make for attached participation in life, and introduced a promethean, and even a "Christian," note into a doctrine which sought the coolness of nirvana through the renunciation of the impulses which impelled to struggle.

There were other concessions. Not merely did compassionate love assert itself, but passionate love made good its claims in those segments of later Buddhism which showed affiliation with Tantrism. Erotic practices were utilized as aids to the attainment of that salvation which proved too difficult for many persons when sought by the technique of self-control and intellectual understanding; surprising doctrines are encountered: "Buddhahood abides in the female organ," "lust is to be crushed by lust," "everything is pure to a pure man." Mysticism also became pronounced in certain of the Buddhist sects. And attempts were made to shorten the attainment of salvation by the increasing introduction of the magical use of Buddhist texts and rituals. In all these ways later Buddhism weakened its allegiance to the principle of detachment from desire, and deviated from the plain but difficult path of the individual seeking salvation by clear understanding and by practice in self-control. Early Buddhism exists in a relatively distinct form in certain regions of Ceylon, Burma, Siam and Cambodia, but it is the later forms of the doctrine which have been dominant in China and Japan; and India, the homeland, has swallowed up Buddhism in the metaphysics, theologies, and rituals which the Buddha had put to one side. The history of Buddhism confirms the predictions attributed to Gautama Buddha that the doctrine would not remain in its pure form for more than five hundred years; and it makes understandable the wish behind the prediction that a new Buddha, Maitreya, the friendly one, should arise in the future to reaffirm the essentials of the doctrine.

It is now time to turn to an assessment of Buddhism. We must distinguish between its general view of the nature of the religious quest and the specific path which Buddhism proposes for the fulfillment of that quest. I should hold that in its conception of the essentially orientational nature of religion, Buddhism had made a contribution of general importance, but that its particular version of the religious life expresses only one type of personality, and is itself not free from ambiguity: there is evidence that the Buddhistic attitude is not adequately expressed as the doctrine of detachment from desire, but that a proper expression of its attitude, though indicated, is not obtained.

The Buddhistic type of person is dominated by the buddhistic (or cerebrotonic) traits of temperament, the dionysian component is weakest, and the promethean component is of intermediate strength. Early Buddhism formulated a way of life congenial in the main to such a person. It stressed self-centeredness, self-sufficiency, solitude, reason; it gave employment to the promethean traits, turning them back upon the individual himself, by encouraging the active techniques for the control of the self which the yoga system of discipline had developed —and this direction was facilitated by the great difficulties in the control of nature encountered in the Indian physical environment; it consistently subordinated the sensual and mystical indulgences which are foreign to temperaments low in dionysian traits, and invoked the full support of ordinary morality to justify this subordination. The Buddha ("supreme charioteer of men to be tamed") gave to such persons the concrete exemplification of a life inherently satisfactory to them—a life alert, poised, calm, self-sufficient; and the attitude of detachment from desire—if taken moderately and not pushed to its absolute extreme—expresses well the attitude to life which such persons inherently find congenial. But by the same token, the Buddhistic path failed to satisfy the orientational needs of other persons;

its path could not maintain itself as *"the* Way"; the changes of attitude represented in the bodhisattva ideal and in the affiliations with Tantrism are attempts by persons higher in promethean and dionysian traits to modify Buddhism in a direction more congenial to their natures.

In this process the ideal of detachment from desire undergoes subtle modifications. And the soil for this modification is prepared in the difficulties encountered in generalizing the attitude of detachment from desire. There is undoubtedly a sense in which the doctrine of detachment is, logically speaking, capable of complete generalization. In principle any specific desire can be weakened or extirpated, and as this is done the individual becomes unconcerned for, "detached from," the objects which this desire would seek for its satisfaction. It is even possible for understanding to be a factor in this process, for in so far as an individual is convinced of the impossibility of satisfying a desire, the desire itself—at least in some cases—seems to be weakened or destroyed. There is no reason why even the desire for detachment cannot be subject to attack, so that one seeks detachment from the desire for detachment itself.

But in this generalization certain unexpected consequences ensue. Understanding seems to weaken or extirpate a desire only by showing the harmful effects of this desire upon some other desire, so that the control of desire (as Spinoza and others have realized) is ultimately by desire and not by understanding alone. Now as long as there is some dominant desire, this can serve as the basis for ordering and controlling other desires, and in early Buddhism the desire for detachment from desire provided this basis. But once let this desire itself weaken, by being applied to itself, and the whole motive power for the attainment or the retention of Buddhist salvation is gone—and we are left simply with the undisciplined and chaotic system of desires that presented the original problem: there is no ground for preferring one desire to another, and the question as to whether we are to seek or retain the state of nirvana is lost in a vague indifferentism. The consistent treader of the path of detachment is a nihilist, and indistinguishable, as we shall see, from his apparent opposite, the consistent Dionysian who attempts to enlarge his attachment to embrace everything whatsoever.

The Buddhist position holds desire to be the distinctive feature of life. If this is so, desire would cease only as life ceased, and death would be the only entrance into nirvana. The fact that the Buddhist condemned suicide, disavowed the dogma of annihilation at death, sought enlightenment, continued to stretch out his alms bowl, and believed that life could continue after the state of nirvana was attained, shows (as does the label of Buddhism as "the middle path") that Buddhism did not push to its extreme the principle of detachment. This is, humanly speaking, to its credit; but it also indicates the inconsistency of a generalized doctrine of detachment from desire with the conception of religion as a way of life attainable by the living. The doctrine gains its strength by not in practice being generalized to include all desire. The only completely detached person is a dead person—and so no person at all.

There is evidence that Buddhistic thought was groping for a formulation of its attitude that would require some union of the ideas of detachment and attachment. Even in early Buddhism we meet with passages that insist that the transcendence of the craving for both existence and nonexistence is not to generate an attitude of indifference; and it is hard to see why one who has not fallen into indifference has not kept some form of "attachment" to something or other. Later Buddhist writings stress that the attitude to nirvana is neither one of attachment nor indifference, and that it is "above affirmation and negation" alike. An interesting section of *The Supreme Path*, called *The Ten Equal Things*, formulates ten doctrines similar to these three:

> For one who is sincerely devoted to the religious life, it is the same whether he refrain from worldly activities or not.
> For him who hath attained the mastery of his mind, it is the same whether he partake of the pleasures of the world or not.
> For him who hath given up the worldly life and taken to the practice of the Spiritual Truths, it is the same whether he observe conventional codes of conduct or not.

Such sayings seem to indicate an attitude of detachment which does not negate ordinary attachments to activity and enjoyment, but which gives to these a unique character in somehow superimposing upon attachment itself a higher level of detachment. We shall return to this suggestion in formulating at a later point the Maitreyan attitude of generalized detached-attachment. For the moment it is only necessary to point out that such sayings give witness that in Buddhism itself the basic attitude sought was not adequately represented in the simple idea of detachment from desire; and they certainly introduce a wedge for promethean and dionysian traits which the simpler formulation and practice tended to exclude.

The Buddhist sought the cause of suffering in the existence and the frustration of desire. Even here two qualifications seem necessary. The satisfaction of a desire is a matter of degree and is a process extending over a period of time. The fact that a desire is frustrated in the sense of not being completely satisfied does not mean that there is no satisfaction in the attempt to secure the desired object or situation. Delay and difficulty in satisfying a desire may even whet the desire and intensify the satisfaction at any stage of the process. Struggle, suffering, pain may themselves in the context of a wider system of desires come to be desired—and such a personality as the Dionysian does in fact desire them. The identification of suffering with the existence and the frustration of desire is not the whole truth, but an evaluation by a particular type of person; it does not plumb the depths of the human self.

The second qualification comes from the fact that desire and its frustration is not the only cause of human woe. Pain has its own direct organs; it may be provoked in the frustration of desire but it need not so arise. The impact of the world on the organism or part of the organism itself may be sufficient to stimulate the nerve cells involved. While pain itself may under certain conditions be desired, the normal desire is to avoid excessive pain, and where the pain is not provoked by the frustration of desire it cannot be controlled by the control of desire. Pain is controlled by changing the conditions of the nerve cells or the forces which act upon them. The method of enlightened self-control can help some individuals to stand or even ignore pain, but it cannot do all. Men are irresistibly impelled to control pain by gaining control of the condition of the organism and the surrounding world. Buddhism cannot here compete with anesthetics: it is no accident that the Buddhist "physicians of the soul" became in many cases physicians of the body, and played their part in the history of Indian medicine. But to turn to such practices is to set foot upon the Promethean path.

The difficulties in generalizing the attitude of detachment; the hidden affirmations involved in the desire for nirvana for oneself and others; the tendency to metaphysical idealism; the introduction of erotic, magical, and mystical practices; the incipient interests in the techniques for objectively controlling the world in which men live; the vague gropings for an attitude of detachment which is not incompatible with some form of attachment: all of these are witnesses in the history of Buddhism to the inadequacies of detachment from desire as an exclusive way of salvation. They demand that we attend to the various paths of attachment which men have followed, and to alternative ways in which the buddhistic traits of human nature have manifested themselves. But while they suggest the inherent inadequacies of the attitude of detachment from desire taken by itself and generalized to the utmost, it does not follow that this attitude is in its entirety to be abandoned. We must not turn from it until we have impressed upon ourselves its sources of strength.

Under the early Buddhist acceptance of detachment from desire lies a mature and enlightened recognition of the fact that human life runs its course in a wider and ultimately more powerful world. Death is inherent in its course, and pain and struggle and frustration. To live in the light of this recognition is to meet the world honestly and realistically. The very recognition is itself a source of strength, for it tempers the outward surge in preparing it to meet obstacles and defeat, and in being foreseen the obstacles and the defeat lose their unexpectedness and something of their power. The individual who has returned to himself as center and taken the reins of life in his own hands is less easy to unseat. The "losing" of the self in the wider world by first contemplating its nature and then reining in its desires is a release from the burden of the self, but it is also a victory for the self since it has met and taken into account its own fate.

Recognition of the difficulty which desires will encounter is a step toward making the self impregnable; the more radical step is to seek freedom from the desires themselves. We have seen that this step cannot without disaster be extended to all desires; that it be extended to some is the counsel of all religions. The ascetic principle has deep roots: the self becomes more manageable as it is simplified; by reducing its demands it makes itself less vulnerable. Since the religious path is for total orientation, it has often sought simplification of the system of desires in the service of such orientation. Its voice is most insistent at those times in which desires have proliferated beyond measure and the conditions of their satisfaction have become precarious. The religious "renunciation of the world" is at heart the search for a simpler, more manageable, more congenial world; the "world" it withdraws from is a society which has become too complex and disorganized. This is a world which is based in the main on possessiveness: on the struggle to attain material goods, social position, objects of love —and emotions and thoughts twist themselves to the service of this struggle. The religious life, commonly though not inevitably, seeks simplification through detachment, and since detachment is nonpossessiveness, it has generally advocated the relinquishment of possessions in property and love, and the purification of thoughts and emotions.

Early Buddhism is unique for the sanity and the thoroughness with which it envisaged the essentials of the religious life. For a moment it permitted men to see, behind the clouds of mythology and metaphysics and perverted asceticism and magical ritual, the religious quest in all its purity. It freed this quest from dependence on the gods, from the question of immortality, from the opposition of the supernatural and the natural, from obedience to dogma and ritual; it placed at the services of this quest enlightened reason and the technique of self-controlled detachment to attain salvation in this life. The essential Buddhism marks one of the great moments in the history of man.

The world today has become complex and disorganized; the religious quest becomes again insistent. It is not likely that the modern religiosity will accept an extreme form of detachment from desire. That it has much to learn from Buddhistic detachment is, however, certain; and in so far as it conceives the essentials of the religious life humanistically and naturalistically it will find deep kinship with the original form of Buddhism. We ourselves will, in a later chapter, attempt this linkage, and avail ourselves of the Buddhist heritage; we will—with apologies to Buddhists if necessary—even use the name of the predicted Buddha to characterize Maitreyan man. If early Buddhism does not supply modern man with a complete path of life, its spirit and its achievements assure that its voice will continue to be heard.

IV. The Dionysian Path of Abandonment

"Yes, my friends, have faith with me in Dionysian life and in the rebirth of tragedy. The time of the Socratic man is past: crown yourselves with ivy, take the thyrsus in your hand, and marvel not if tigers and panthers lie down fawning at your feet. Dare now to be tragic men, for ye shall be redeemed! Ye shall accompany the Dionysian festive procession from India to Greece! Arm yourselves for hard strife, but have faith in the wonders of your god!"

Nietzsche:
The Birth of Tragedy

IV

The Dionysian Path of Abandonment

LIFE involves desire, attachment, struggle. Men and women in all ages and in diverse ways have celebrated their attachment to life, their affirmation of its countless forms, their intoxication in victory and defeat. They have stopped at no means to heighten their sense of living, to fill the cup of life to the full, to sing of "the many flowery islands" which "lie in the waters of wide agony," to raise this agony itself to a source of insight. And when this passion to plunge with abandon into the waters of elemental life becomes a center of orientation, it takes on the form of a religion, and invokes its god, Dionysus.

The Greek god Dionysus was a god of vegetation, of wine, of passionate love, of the theater; his symbols were the ivy, the thyrsus, the panther, the vine; he was celebrated in dramatic festivals as the deliverer of men from winter and the herald of spring's eternal renewal of life; in eating the raw flesh of the sacrificial ox his worshipers symbolically renewed their life in and through the death of their god; his perpetual death and resurrection has become the symbol of wild abandon to the great demonic affirmation of life. In *The Bacchae* of Euripides we still can hear something of the voice of Dionysian Greece in which blend the note of joy and the fierce wild cry of anguished ecstasy. Frenzied shouts, the cruel dismemberment of the sacrificial animal, the communion of blood, phallic rituals, wine, dances, the flare of torches at the night rituals:— the frenzied blaze of life flaming in the darkness of death.

It will become evident that Dionysianism is a particular version of attachment; it is by no means an attachment to all phases of life. The legend of Orpheus is instructive at this point. Orphism was a peculiar development within the cult of Dionysus; it had an ascetic element and a stress on sanity and moderation. The legend runs that Orpheus had paid his favors to the sun, to Apollo, as the greatest god, and that Dionysus, furious at this blasphemy, had sent his followers to dismember Orpheus and strew his parts far and wide. Apollo we will meet again—as a god of light, of clarity, of ethical moderation, he represented the forces of stable culture; Dionysianism on the contrary voiced the generative and demonic forces of nature and human nature; it is akin to mystic communion with the elemental, it is ill at ease when far from blood, it is essentially the paean of untamed life. It is the return of anguished life from the bonds of organized society to its biological heritage and its cosmic fate. It is the frenzied affirmation of the primal agony of man itself, whipped up by wine and lust and cruelty. It is as hostile to the socializing, civilizing, taming elements of human culture as it is to the Buddhistic life of detachment from desire. In it life forces itself from the late burden of the social and moral self to affirm its older nature, to celebrate the sources of its power, its struggles, its annihilation, its renewal. Joy in struggle intertwined with death, joy in the insurgence of untamed life, joy in mergence with the forces which kill and renew: such joy—fierce, anguished, ecstatic— is the goal, the salvation, of the votary of Dionysus.

In the nature of the case, the Dionysian is not inclined to "present his case" before the bar of the mind. He is operative in all peoples and in all individuals, but he is felt more often than heard. We can best track him to his lair in the writings of Nietzsche, who refers to himself as "the last disciple and initiate of the god Dionysus." In this complex personality there are crosscurrents to be sure, and these we must not neglect; but we shall not go far wrong in regarding his *Zarathustra* as the bible of Dionysianism and his prose writings as its apologetics. Nietzsche used Christ and Schopenhauer as the foils for his own views, and we can approach the core of his Dionysianism through those whom he took to be his arch enemies.

The essence of Nietzsche's critique of Christianity lies in his interpretation of it as "Buddhistic," as life-denying, and in his attempt to show that this attitude is only a mask for a hidden and degenerate Dionysianism in which the "weak" and the sick affirm and celebrate their own weakness, sickness, suffering, and hate of the "strong." In the fury of his attack on Christianity we witness a struggle (within Nietzsche and within Western culture) between two emphases of the Dionysian components of personality. That this struggle involves a distortion of both Buddha and Christ is to be expected; Nietzsche is a religious prophet and not a writer of historical treatises. Has he not proclaimed that "to enable a sanctuary to be set up *a sanctuary has to be destroyed*"? We must not forget the characterization he gives of himself in *Ecce Homo*:

> I know the joy of *annihilation* to a degree commensurate with my power to annihilate. In both cases I obey my Dionysian nature, which cannot separate the negative deed from yea-saying. I am the first immoralist, and thus I am the essential destroyer.

Nietzsche's attack on Christianity is simultaneously an attack on Schopenhauer, whose discovery had been a major event in the course of Nietzsche's own development. Schopenhauer is the witness of an important stage in European culture: he marks the introduction of Buddhist elements into the Christian tradition of the West. The image of Buddha sat on his desk, and the Buddhistic way of life is unmistakable in his writings.

Schopenhauer couched his views under the central concept of "the will to live." The fourth part of his main work, *The World as Will and Idea*, deals with "The Assertion and Denial of the Will to Live." The doctrine of the will to live is essentially the extension to all things of the view that the essence of life is desire, and the consequent personification of the world as a Will doomed to eternal struggle and to the suffering imposed by frustration of desire. The life of each individual, as one manifestation of the universal Will, is accordingly a tragedy: the individual seeks "a chimerical happiness in an ephemeral, dream-like, and delusive existence," and yet he meets "fate visibly directed to the mortification of our will and the abolition of the illusion that holds us chained in the bonds of this world."

Two emphases open to the individual are familiar to us as the release or the restraint of desire; Schopenhauer calls these the affirmation of the will to live and the denial of the will to live. He interprets Buddhism and Christianity as forms of the latter: Buddhist nirvana is envisaged as the denial of the will to live; the Christian doctrine of original sin is equated with the assertion of the will, while the denial of the will—"the one great truth which constitutes the essence of Christianity"— is identified with the Christian ideal of salvation. Schopenhauer presented his own views as the philosophical formulation of the essentials of Indian and Christian religions.

The path of denial which he indicates is likewise Buddhistic and Christian, and more the latter than the former. He admits with the Buddhist that knowledge of the will and the conditions of human life weakens the will to live, but he believes that suffering itself is the effective and central agency: pain is the "purifying lye" of life; the cross is the symbol of Christianity. And love but increases the urgency of pain. Erotic love does this, in its own way, but even more so Christian love, in which one takes on the suffering of others almost as vividly as one undergoes one's own suffering. And, so we are told, this disinterested love for others, this extension of suffering, weakens further the aggressive concern for oneself, and leads to salvation, to the entire surrender of the will to live, to the relinquishment "of all volition." In the disinterestedness of knowledge, in the disinterestedness of art, and above all in the disinterestedness of love, the self saps its own attachment to existence and cuts the roots of its will to live.

Schopenhauer had thus brought into prominence Christian means in reaching the Buddhist goal. It is as though the fixing of attention upon suffering through knowledge and art and sympathetic love somehow weakened the aggressive impulses upon which suffering depends. There is a paradox in this which Nietzsche will exploit to the full: detachment is to be attained by a supposedly temporary attachment to suffering itself; one is to carry the cross of life so that one's will to live may be crucified upon it.

In Schopenhauer the West had finally met the East. Its aggressive promethean surge had encountered the specter of annihilation: the annihilation of the individual will to live, and the annihilation of even the cosmic will to live. The last paragraph of *The World as Will and Idea* carries us into the presence of late Buddhist doctrines of the void. Even the phenomenal world—the world of nature—is regarded as an "objectification" of the will, and vanishes as the will is negated.

"Before us there is certainly only nothingness":—to will our nothingness, to yoke love itself to the will to nothingness, to will cosmic nothingness: such is the ultimate counsel of this nineteenth century apostle of a Buddhistically transformed Christianity.

In Christianity and in Schopenhauer Nietzsche saw the shadow cast by a coming nihilism: a Europe embracing a new Buddhism, a disintegrating Europe heading for the abyss of nothingness, celebrating and even willing its own disintegration. His onslaught on Christianity was an attempt to diagnose the nature of this will to nothingness; the attack on morality, science, democracy, socialism, communism, was to show the forms of corruption to which this will had led; and this attack and onslaught were themselves but preliminaries to the positive goal: the supplanting of the will to nothingness by a new affirmative will opening a new channel for the repressed and belittled energies of mankind.

Nietzsche accepted the view that life by its nature is interested life. Life is dynamic, aggressive, ever passing on from one attainment to new demands; Nietzsche baptizes this tendency as "the will to power." He extends it to things at large; the world is interpreted as a constant struggle between active centers of power to increase their power. This struggle involves suffering and it often encounters defeat. In the sphere of organic beings there is—so the account runs—a basic opposition between the weak, the sick, the fatigued, the ill-constituted organisms, and the strong, the healthy, the exuberant, the well-constituted ones. Each seeks the maximum of power, but the forms of the will and therefore the principles of valuation

differ in the two cases: those of deficient energy seek security
from the world and their more powerful opponents, their
frustrated longings fester in resentment of themselves and the
world, they seek release from the struggle; those of overflowing energy, on the contrary, seek an unsettled world which
they can bind to themselves, gratitude accompanies the release
of their powers, struggle itself is welcomed and affirmed. It is
in the clash between these two types of natures that Nietzsche
reads the history of man and his future. Against the life-
denying Nay of the weak he sets the life-affirming Yea of the
strong.

But since life—all life—is seen as a will to power, it is in-
cumbent upon Nietzsche to unmask ascetic ideals, and to show
that the will to nothingness yet remains a will. The attack is
not on all forms of this ideal (in so far as asceticism is frankly
an instrument of discipline and the ascetic life a search—as in
the case of the philosopher—for an environment in which a
dominant affirmative interest can seek its optimum discharge,
the ascetic life is extolled in Nietzsche) but on the ascetic ideal
in so far as it becomes life-denying—and this he takes to be
the case in Christianity, and Buddhism, and in their Schopen-
hauerian reflection. In such cases the path of detachment is regarded as a perverted form of attachment: sickness, weakness,
suffering are themselves extolled as positive goods and their
possessors as ideal persons; passion, cruelty, power, possessions, audacity—all that makes for involvement in "the world"
—are condemned; the repressed and frustrated will to power
pictures to itself a "Kingdom to come" in which it will be
supreme, and assumes the language of love, which Nietzsche
here interprets as pity to fellow sufferers and as a hidden but
implacable hate for all healthy and overflowing natures. The
sufferers band together for strength, and such an organization

is the Church; the priest is the herdsman of the flock, making a virtue out of suffering, enticing the sheep with visions of a new day to come, and directing the hidden war against their natural enemies. Democracy, socialism, communism are regarded as progressive victories in this war. The morality which stresses neighborly love, moderation, social utility, happiness, is interpreted as voicing the ideals of the herd. Science itself is interpreted as a form of the ascetic ideal: an asceticism of the intellect in which the living being trains himself until he becomes simply a mirror that reflects whatever occurs.

Nietzsche sees one direction involved in these religious, political, and intellectual forces: a movement by which the weak and sick bind together for the leveling of differences between men, for the taming and domestication and impoverishment of human nature.

> The gregarious European man nowadays assumes an air as if he were the only kind of man that is allowable; he glorifies his qualities, such as public spirit, kindness, deference, industry, temperance, modesty, indulgence, sympathy, by virtue of which he is gentle, endurable, and useful to the herd, as the peculiarly human virtues.

Nietzsche conceived of the philosopher as the creator of values, as "the Caesarean trainer and dictator of civilization." What is Nietzsche's counterwill to the will of nothingness? We have seen that this will to nothingness was itself regarded by Nietzsche as a hidden affirmation by weak struggling life of its yet remaining powers; it is therefore at heart a "cult of suffering," a Dionysianism of the masses, life—though weak life—celebrating its pain and yet seeking salvation from this pain in indulging it, in withdrawing from the "world," and in resentment and hostility (disguised as love) to the strong. Nietzsche's counterwill is likewise Dionysian—but a Dionysianism in which the frustrated and self-directed dionysian impulses are liberated and turned outward. It erects what it takes to be the basic fact of life (that life seeks power, seeks to discharge its strength) into the norm for life: the man of overflowing vitality and exuberance is to take himself as norm: what makes for his power is good; what lessens his power is evil. Suffering too is good, but suffering as discipline, as matrix for the summoning of life's resources, not as end. Knowledge, art, love are good, once they are pressed into the service of affirmative life and their "disinterestedness" refuted. Cruelty, passion, hatred, hardness, jealousy, war are involved in the struggle for power, and accepted. The morality of mediocrity and utility is opposed by a morality of daring, of aggressiveness, of delight in life as appropriation and exploitation. The summons is to bold and free individuals who are to carve a table of values for the "higher man" out of the debris of the shattered monuments of the bourgeois and proletarian society.

Some day, in a stronger age than this rotting and introspective present, must he in sooth come to us, even the *redeemer* of great love and scorn, the creative spirit, rebounding by the impetus of his own force back again away from every transcendental plane and dimension, he whose solitude is misunderstood by the people, as though it were a flight *from* reality; —while actually it is only his diving, burrowing, and penetrating *into* reality, so that when he comes again to the light he can at once bring about by these means the *redemption* of this reality; its redemption from the curse which the old ideal has laid upon it. This man of the future, who in this wise will redeem us from the old ideal, as he will from that ideal's necessary corollary of great nausea, will to nothingness, and Nihilism; this tocsin of noon and of the great verdict, which renders the will again free, who gives back to the world its goal and to man his hope, this Antichrist and Antinihilist, this conqueror of God and of Nothingness—*he must one day come.*

The counterwill is expected to meet its enemies—the holders-on of the dying bourgeois culture and the advancing proletariat—in the open field. This meant to Nietzsche great wars in the struggle for the control of man and the earth; it meant opposition to the whole parliamentary procedure of democratic-capitalistic culture; it meant conflict to the death with the rising communistic culture.

Nietzsche was aware that this counterwill might not prevail, but he was not without hope that it would. As one who saw struggle as the condition under which life was forced to develop its resources, he thought that the conflict between the aristocratic and the plebeian tables of values (between "master" and "slave" morality) which had dominated the history of Europe had produced a "magnificent tension," and that "with such a tensely strained bow one can now aim at the furthest goals." He even thought that the conditions in Europe making for the extension of the will to nothingness favored also the appearance of new aggressive "blond beasts": "The democratising of Europe will tend to the production of a type prepared for *slavery* in the most subtle sense of the term," and equally well to "the rearing of *tyrants*—taking the word in all its meaning, even in its most spiritual sense." The clash of ideologies, economies, and armies in the world today is evidence that Nietzsche's pen was dipped in the ink of living cultural realities.

It is easy to scorn this doctrine or embrace it enthusiastically —this requires merely the letting out of one's own religious attitude; it is difficult to penetrate to its roots. It is suggested that we find the cue in Nietzsche's own designation of himself in *Beyond Good and Evil* as "the last disciple and initiate of the god Dionysus." Let us follow this cue.

Nietzsche has delineated the Dionysian attitude in detail, especially in *The Birth of Tragedy* and in *Beyond Good and Evil*. It is a state akin to drunkenness, it involves the forgetfulness of self and the celebration of the reunion of man and nature, it is barbaric and titanic, it is an enchantment with the immediate sensuous dynamic features of life and nature. The Dionysian attitude is contrasted by Nietzsche to the Apollonian attitude which stresses sunlike clarity, freedom from wild emotions, self-knowledge, measured restraint, philosophical calm, an ethical orientation; in terms of this contrast we see that the Dionysian seeks relief from the burden of the social and self-controlled self through abandon to the more elemental phases of the self. It is thus an attachment to life in its essential and pervasive features, and hostile at once to the ascetic denial of life and the complications of the self and its controls which civilization imposes. The self seeks in the Dionysian attitude to free itself from restraint, to replenish itself by the plunge into the elemental forms of life. This attitude thus reveals itself as an affirmation of life, but not the whole of life; it is an uneasy life which seeks release from the burden of the social self; the note of sadness which haunts its joy reveals a frantic core underlying its frenzied affirmation.

The Dionysian attitude contains an essentially dramatic element. Dionysus was the patron of the theater; Nietzsche tried to show that the Greek tragedy was the portrayal in an Apollonian art form of the Dionysian wisdom, that this might be contemplated and endured. In such tragedy man saw his kinship with nature, and in witnessing his fate learned to assimilate it, to accept it, and to celebrate it. Dionysianism raises to the level of a dramatic spectacle the affirmation of life, its struggle, its tragic fate, and its perpetual renewal.

In all these respects Nietzsche is a true votary of Dionysus. He attacks equally the ascetic ideal and a morally, scientifically, technologically oriented culture. He defends the impulses of human nature which these ideals and this culture seek to control or subdue. Against comfort, fatigue, restraint, detachment, irresolution, resentment, he preaches the seduction of a bold, wanton, abandoned life trusting its elemental sources and its untried possibilities. The language is intoxicating, dramatic, unsettling, challenging—the language of an "equivocator and tempter," to use the words he applied to Dionysus. It is the language of the religious prophet attempting to inculcate in man a basic attitude—the attitude of Dionysianism. To be a tragedian, composing with man as material a Dionysian tragedy: that is Nietzsche's deepest impulse. A Dionysian festival extended to the whole of human life—to, indeed, the whole cosmos: that is his hidden content and theme.

Such an interpretation of Nietzsche as basically Dionysian, seeing in life the content of a Dionysian festival and desiring to impose on life the form of a Greek tragedy, is only part of the story; it requires supplementation and sharpening of focus by recognition of the place which Nietzsche gives to the promethean and buddhistic traits of personality, even though these remain subordinated to the dionysian trait.

The Dionysian emphasis is only in apparent contradiction to the Promethean facet of his personality: his interest in transforming the table of values of mankind from a "slave" to a "master" basis. Nietzsche had been nourished on the titans of Greek tragedy; he did not like the modern actors in mankind's play: the hero was lacking and he wished to reintroduce him on the Greek mold. And this to improve the play: no more, no less. That the Promethean motive is controlled by the preference for a Dionysian type of life and type of hero may be brought out in various ways.

One line of evidence is indicated by Nietzsche's interpretation of the Promethean myth itself. In Nietzsche the figures of Prometheus and Dionysus tend to coalesce and each to take on characteristics usually reserved for the other. In *The Birth of Tragedy* Dionysus is said to share with Prometheus "the titanic impulse to become as it were the Atlas of all individuals, and on broad shoulders to bear them higher and higher"; while "active sin"—represented in the theft of fire from the gods—is taken to be "the essential Promethean virtue." Prometheus is in this way made an "immoralist," and his titanic revolt against existing conditions is given precedence over the socially motivated and technologically directed activity commonly in the forefront of the Promethean myth. While Dionysus borrows something from Prometheus in this interchange, the net result is the assimilation of Prometheus to the image of Dionysus.

That underlying Nietzsche's Promethean crusade there is a preference for the Dionysian type of man, hidden in what seems at first to be an objective classification of men into "weak" and "strong," can be brought out by criticism of his doctrine of the will to power. This doctrine is itself a dramatic and mythological rendering of the fact that life is essentially interested action. There is no scientific evidence of a single "will to power" of which each particular interest is a special instance; "will to power" seems to add nothing to the statement that men are interested beings and that each interest by its very nature

seeks satisfaction. For this reason there can be no general classification of men into "weak" and "strong": the strength of a person can only be measured relative to the persistence of specific interests and their capacity to secure objects by which they can
be satisfied. And by this criterion any type of person can be
"strong"; approval or disapproval of the type of person must
rest on other grounds. Those that Nietzsche disapproved of—
and confusedly calls "weak"—are, if his own analysis be correct, very "strong." The "slaves," the "masses," have on this
analysis practically taken control of mankind; if amount of
power is the criterion of value then these "strong ones" are the
"good ones." If the answer be that *individually* these persons
are "weak," this answer has its answer: a person who can unite
with others in a way to secure his ends is, on any intelligible
use of terms, a "strong" person. "Power," "weakness,"
"strength"—these terms are in Nietzsche's mouth terms of approval and disapproval, not terms of description. They are the
words of an "equivocator," used by a "tempter," a fisher of
men, as means of seduction to his preferred type of man: to the
tragic hero, the actor in the grand manner, to Dionysus.

It was a decisive and disturbing moment in Nietzsche's life
when the recognition forced itself upon him that this type of
man needed as his complement, as his material, the "Christian"
type of man upon which Nietzsche had turned his venom,—
and that, accordingly, Christian man too had to be affirmed! As
a Promethean "moralist" Nietzsche could take sides; as a
Dionysian he was forced to affirm the conditions under which
his chosen type of man was made possible and could operate.
The "weak" had to be accepted and affirmed as well as the
"strong"; the "slaves" as well as the "masters." And in the
conflict the Dionysian Nietzsche overcomes the Promethean
moralist; the doctrine of eternal recurrence takes precedence

over the doctrine of the superman. For the doctrine that all that occurs has occurred in all its details endlessly in the past and will reoccur endlessly in the future was more than an objective doctrine for Nietzsche: its acceptance was an acceptance of all existence (the "weak" and the petty along with the "strong" and sublime) and all struggle; its acceptance meant the unqualified affirmation of life and its conditions. In this way Nietzsche has generalized and extended to the utmost the Dionysian attitude. In his own way he had attained salvation; he had done for himself what he felt had been the miracle of Greek tragedy: the presentation of life's eternal struggle and renewal in a form in which this struggle and renewal could be contemplated, endured, and affirmed. Just as Buddhism in its development showed the influx of promethean and dionysian factors, so does this generalized Dionysianism contain not only a vein of prometheanism; it knows the value of detachment as well:

Not to cleave to any person, be it even the dearest—every person is a prison and also a recess. Not to cleave to a fatherland, be it even the most suffering and necessitous—it is even less difficult to detach one's heart from a victorious fatherland. Not to cleave to a sympathy, be it even for higher men, into whose peculiar torture and helplessness chance has given us an insight. Not to cleave to a science, though it tempt one with the most valuable discoveries, apparently specially reserved for *us*. Not to cleave to one's own liberation, to the voluptuous distance and remoteness of the bird, which always flies further aloft in order always to see more under it—the danger of the flier. Not to cleave to our own virtues, nor become as a whole a victim to any of our specialties, to our "hospitality" for instance, which is the danger of dangers for highly developed and wealthy souls, who deal prodigally, almost indifferently with themselves, and push the virtue of liberality so far that

it becomes a vice. One must know how *to conserve oneself*—
the best test of independence.

In putting life on the stage as a spectacle one becomes a spectator of oneself as actor. And in Nietzsche, the advocate of
the higher man and of struggle, there appears the note of the
divine spectator, in the struggle but elevated beyond it, freed
from suffering with the higher man, freed from resentment of
the lower man, freed even from one's elevation, "without a
yea or a nay for reality save that from time to time one acknowledges it after the manner of a good dancer, with the tips
of one's toes." And yet this detachment is clearly in the service
of Dionysus, that the Dionysian world-festival be lifted to the
highest conscious intensity. From the lips of Zarathustra there
sounds the intoxicated voice of Dionysus: "The world is
perfect!"

The Dionysian type of person is dominated by dionysian
traits, buddhistic traits are nevertheless very strong, and promethean traits lowest of all. The conflict between detachment
and indulgence inherent in such a personality is periodically
resolved—perhaps with the help of wine—by a dissipation of
the tension in the explosive release of the dionysian traits; the
high buddhistic and low promethean characteristics give a distinctive form to the release: it becomes a festival outside the
round of the normal social life, intense and dramatic and impersonal in character, centering around the more elemental biologic appetites. The conflict of the components of personality
produces the anguish, the suffering, the ecstasy associated with
the Dionysian festival. Personalities in which the dionysian
component is highest but the buddhistic low in strength do not

manifest this conflict; we shall find this is true of the Moham-medan type of personality; Omar Khayyam could serve as an example of a milder Dionysianism. The earlier accounts of Dionysus in Greece have the accent of a gay agricultural com-munity enjoying the normal release of ordinary human interests prefigured in the ending of winter and the beginning of spring's tumult; only later is Dionysus endowed with the more frenzied personality which we have distinguished as Dionysian and can discern in the drama of Euripides.

We have argued that the key to the interpretation of Nietzsche is to be found in the preference for the Dionysian personality. Nietzsche is certainly the champion of the dionysian phase of human nature, and his preferred type fits more nearly the Dionysian than any other type. The qualifications which this statement requires arise from the fact that Nietzsche is operating with a simplified theory of personality in which he emphasizes three types: the Dionysian, the Christian, the Apol-lonian. It is the conflict of the first two which is essential to his account; the only real function apparently provided for the Apollonian is to insure that the Dionysian attitude enjoy itself aesthetically. As a result of this oversimplification, Nietzsche blurs the distinction between the Christian and Buddhist types (as Schopenhauer had done) and gives traits to the Dionysian which a more detailed classification would ascribe to the Pro-methean and the Mohammedan. It is this fact which makes it so difficult to get a sharp picture of the type of man which Nietzsche intends to champion; Spengler, among others, has insisted that Nietzsche is precise in terms of what he opposes and vague as to what he proposes.

Clarity is obtained if we recognize that the Christians, Bud-dhists, and Apollonians agree in one feature: they are all re-strainers of the dionysian impulses within the limits of a socially

approved morality; in contrast, the Dionysians, the Prometheans, and the Mohammedans are releasers of impulses
which threaten to upset the institutions of established society.
Nietzsche is really opposing the releasers en bloc to the re-
strainers en bloc, and championing the first group as against the
second. It is in these terms that his contrast between the
"strong" and the "weak" is to be interpreted, and his opposition of himself as an "immoralist" to all previous "moralists."
And this is the reason why Nietzsche at once appeals irresistibly
to all creators, and yet has been used by very diverse persons as
the advocate of what they themselves so variously advocate.
The Promethean, the Dionysian, the Mohammedan can all dip
their pitchers in his well. He releases the releasers—even to
warfare on each other.

Once the relevant distinctions have been made, I believe it is
just to say that Nietzsche is best envisaged as the advocate of
Dionysian man. The only other plausible view is to regard his
"higher man" as a hesitant and confused prefigurement of
Maitreyan man. We shall see that this type of person is characterized by a strong amount of all three components of temperament. We have noted that in one way or another all of
these components attain in Nietzsche a place, even though they
are—somewhat unconvincingly—wrapped in the Dionysian
robe. Give them their proper balance, bring them to a just
focus—and Zarathustra would begin to look at us through the
eyes of Maitreya. But then the restrainers would not all be on
the wrong side and the releasers all on the right side; and the
dramatic but easy oppositions of the "weak" and the "strong,"
the "slaves" and the "masters," the "body" and the "reason,"
the "individual" and the "social," the "moralists" and the "im-
moralists" would have to be assigned to the limbo to which—
for the Maitreyan—they belong.

Certain it is that Nietzsche mirrored in himself the major conflicts of personality found in Western culture. His own struggles focus the struggle of this culture to define a type of man to which allegiance can be given; it is less surprising that he went down in this struggle than that he lasted as long as he did. If Nietzsche did not formulate this type he at least hammered at the stone, and he did champion in an irrefutable way the rights of the dionysian phase of the self to be allowed expression. Since his day a multitude of voices have gained courage to speak in the name of this phase of the self. Nietzsche thought that "all religions are mainly concerned with fighting a certain fatigue and heaviness that has infected everything." He worked as a releaser from such fatigue and heaviness; in terms of his own conception of religion he is essentially a religious figure. He has gained the right to speak as the modern exemplar of the ancient god Dionysus.

The Buddhistic path attempts to conquer suffering by extirpating its causes through understanding; the Dionysian path attempts to wring joy from suffering by participating in suffering and accepting its conditions. To affirm suffering itself, to raise it to intense consciousness, to find it an aesthetic source of joy—this is another stratagem by which man has met his agony. There is a tonic effect in this plunge back into the waters of essential life, a mystic joy in this re-establishment of the continuity of the individual life with the cosmic play of things, a sense of liberation in this letting go of the self—even to its annihilation. There are demonic forces in human nature that strain at restraint and demand their day. There are obstacles in the path of every creative one which drive him back to the determined affirmation of his deepest impulses if the obstacles are to be surmounted. There is an inherent cruelty in every specific form of love which insists on realizing its goal in the face of competing loves with competing goals—destruction is verily the prelude to creation. There is a purifying quality in pain, and strength in accepting and embracing the struggle and suffering inevitable to a life of attachment. To fail to see clearly these matters is to look upon life with superficial eyes. The sources of Dionysianism go deep, and water from this well will always be sought.

And yet the water is seldom clear or completely satisfying to most types of personality. For affirmation, attachment, is a matter of degree, and the forms of suffering are as manifold as the forms of desire. If the attachment is to selected objects, Dionysianism itself gives no principle of selection; if the attachment is to the biologic self, other phases of the self protest; if the attachment is impartially extended to everything, Dionysianism furnishes no principle for specific action—in affirming everything it would lose the ground for affirming anything against anything else. Hence—as we have seen—it tends to borrow nourishment from other forms of the religious quest (as they in turn borrow from it): detachment in some form makes its entry and some specific promethean impulse makes its bid for allegiance. So it is that Dionysianism suggests—as did Buddhism—a need for a more comprehensive form of the religious quest.

The self which in the historic manifestations of Dionysianism has sought relief from its burden in the affirmation and assumption of this burden has been, by and large, the biologic self ill at ease in the jacket wrought by the existing form of society. In affirming this biologic self it has tended to repudiate the social self which has been built upon and around it.

Dionysus has been a jealous god, hostile to morality, to science, to technology, to the life of reason; he has tried to unmask any form of love which did not reduce the object of love to an impersonal means to the satisfaction of one's own desire. The Dionysian affirmation of the self has not been the affirmation of the whole complex self which occasions the human agony; and this incompleteness is the explanation of its uneasy and anguished joy, and its ever-present tendency to make of suffering a cult. The self that escapes its full burden in some Dionysian festival—be it a festival of war or passion or suffering or wine —attains the exhilaration of release, but its full heart is likely to remain unsatisfied. Siva has required Brahma and Vishnu as his complements; destruction is but the prelude to creation and preservation. Other gods than Dionysus demand to be heard.

Nietzsche distorted Buddhism in seeing it simply as the will to nothingness; he distorted the historic Christ in seeing him as a Hellenized Christ whose love was disguised resentment against the "strong" and whose mission was to glorify the suffering of the "weak." The Nietzschean Christ is a perverted Dionysus, and the Nietzschean Antichrist was to be the regained Dionysus. And yet the very intensity of this struggle arouses a query as to the genuineness of this opposition, and the legitimacy of his battle cry: "Dionysus or Christ!" There are passages which reveal an attitude of affection for Christ, as though Nietzsche's warfare was a struggle within himself. Christ is presented as one of great love who had failed to find an object worthy of this love; and Christian love, though thought to ground in hate, is characterized as "the most perfect and sublime of all forms of love." In Nietzsche's *Night Song* there wells up from dark lonely waters the fountain of a great love—a great unsatisfied love forced to seek solace in its own depths, and craving hatred and destruction of self and others out of its own intensity. This is the picture Nietzsche consciously drew of Christ, and involuntarily of himself, "The Crucified One." "Dionysus *or* Christ?" or "Dionysus *and* Christ?" And other gods as well? Was not Nietzsche more complex, more profound, more tempting, than his formula?

Dionysus was for Nietzsche himself the symbol of "the religious affirmation of life, the whole of life, not of denied and partial life." And Nietzsche demands a god that is "the whole of the abundant assembly of life's contrasts, *saving* and *justifying* them in a divine agony." Is Dionysus in Nietzsche's hands perhaps the mask, the distortion, the disguise, the foreboding— of Maitreyan man?

V. The Promethean Path of Unceasing Making

"Yea, in fennel stalk
I snatched the hidden spring of stolen fire,
Which is to men a teacher of all arts,
Their chief resource. And now, this penalty
Of that offence I pay, fast riveted
In chains beneath the open firmament."

Prometheus, in Aeschylus:
Prometheus Bound

"See, the man has become like one of us, in knowing good from evil; and now, suppose he were to reach out his hand and take the fruit of the tree of life also, and eating it, live forever! So the Lord God expelled him from the Garden of Eden, to till the ground from which he had been taken; he drove the man out, and stationed the Cherubs east of the Garden of Eden, with the flaming, whirling sword to guard the way to the tree of life."

Genesis 3:22-24

"Were the naturalistic foundations and bearings of religion grasped, the religious element in life would emerge from the throes of the crisis in religion. Religion would then be found to have its natural place in every aspect of human experience that is concerned with estimate of possibilities, with emotional stir by possibilities as yet unrealized, and with all action in behalf of their realization."

John Dewey:
A Common Faith

V

The Promethean Path of Unceasing Making

MAN is not merely viscera and cerebrum: he is also an elaborate musculature eventuating in crafty and restless hands. He has dared to invade his living and nonliving environment to take from it what he needed, and to change it to the end that he might take more. He has built up auxiliary mechanisms so that his vision might be extended, his arm stronger, his grasp tighter. He has made over his world, only to remake it over again and again. Driven back by too strong forces at one point, he has attacked at another. He conquered his larger animal competitors; he battled his human rivals; he raped his Earth Mother. He has known struggle, war, defeat, victory in his unceasing making. He has shown courage, inventiveness, craftiness, resourcefulness, defiance, pride. He has contemplated his activity in the image of Prometheus.

Prometheus was one of the Titans, progenies of gods and men. He stole fire from the gods to place it at the service of man. For this, Zeus caused him to be chained to a mountain, and vultures picked by day at his liver which healed by night. Prometheus remained defiant in suffering, hopeful as to the future, proud of the forces which he had released.

The Promethean myth presents the symbol of the maker, accepting as actuality the whole pack of insurgent human desires, defiant of hostile powers, assuming willingly the suffering his activity entails, striving to command the techniques by which man may improve his lot. Prometheus is primarily technologist:

various forms of the myth attribute to him the gifts of building, of navigation, of mining, of divination, of medicine. But reasoning was also among his gifts; his name signifies forethought, he introduced the alphabet, he gave men knowledge of the seasons and the stars, he brought men numbers and counting, his name was often linked with that of Athena the goddess of wisdom. Devoted to the interests of men, guided by knowledge, skilled in the technical arts: this is the figure of the mythological Prometheus.

It should be noted that there is nothing inherently social in promethean activity as such, nor any necessity that this activity be motivated by love of mankind. And yet in the Promethean myth these elements are more and more incorporated: they are hardly noticeable in Hesiod's *Theogony*, visible in Aeschylus' *Prometheus Bound*, more prominent in Goethe's utilization of the Faustian legend, and made dominant in Shelley's *Prometheus Unbound*. It is not difficult to see why a socially directed love becomes so incorporated into the figure of Prometheus. The promethean activity of the self, even if desired on its own account, is an activity which seeks satisfaction of whatever interests are in fact existent, and the acceptance of these interests is to this degree a form of love, though an indiscriminate form by no means to be confused with Christian love or with a moral orientation of the personality: given any interest, the strongly promethean personality will simply set about to secure the agencies for its satisfaction. But now it turns out, as a matter of fact, that the most effective agencies—such as science and machine technology—require co-operation and the funding of social experience; the promethean technologist becomes in this way embedded in the cultural context which supports effective technological endeavor. He even attains in this process a moral justification for his activities. But we must not fail to see that the essential feature of the Promethean personality resides in the continual reconstruction of the world in the service of whatever desires in fact obtain—and the love of mankind, morality, science are themselves but possible channels for his unceasing making.

The myth of the fall of man varies the emphasis of the Promethean myth but keeps unchanged the main motive. It is now man himself who, in Adam, dares to possess for himself blessings reserved for the gods. It is his passions, symbolized as passion for woman, which impel him to his deed; and the fruit of the deed is knowledge—though now especially knowledge of good and evil. The technological element of the Promethean myth is in the background, though indicated in the condemning of man to till the soil, and in the fear of the gods that man, having tasted of knowledge, will seek the fruits of the second tree, the tree of life itself; the change in emphasis brings to the forefront the note of morality, but does not destroy the picture of man taking his destiny in his own hands, remaining true to his own vital interests, daring to seek actively a fuller and untried life, and accepting the suffering which flows from such activity.

The Greek and the Semitic myths bear witness to the daring, the fear, and the hesitation with which man has taken his destiny into his restless hands; in their expanded form they show the pain which has been involved in the growth of the social self and in the progressive assumption of a moral orientation to life and its technological implementation. The superimposition of a social self upon man's biological heritage, and the constant interpenetration and modification of these sources of human desire, have produced the deepest conflict which human nature has had to bear. This conflict, as well as man's daring and fear and hesitation in launching himself upon his own, are reflected in the myths of the fire bringer and the fall of man. The Promethean core of these myths has supplied content for countless writers, painters, musicians of the West. This core, systematized and clarified, is the Promethean path of the maker; this Promethean religion has been the essential religion of Western man.

The *Faust* of Goethe exhibits the struggle of the Promethean temperament to free itself from alien temperaments and to attain its own pure form. In taking us behind the scenes into the formation of the Promethean attitude, and in disclosing the essential motives and difficulties of this temperament, the *Faust* stands as the bible of Prometheanism.

We meet the restless, tormented, dissatisfied Faust at the moment in which he turns away from the gray detachment involved in the quest for knowledge to plunge as a child of the earth into the green turmoil of human life. It is early made clear that Faust is to take the path of action ("In the beginning was the *Deed*!" "Only restlessly active is a man!") ; but a life of a hundred years is necessary for him to define and clarify this path until the essentially Promethean character of his attitude is recognized and purified. The pact with Mephistopheles but determines the larger framework: Faust will relinquish his soul to the Devil at that instant in which he rests self-satisfied on "the bed of sloth," wishing to bind some moment of achievement and consummation with the exclamation, "Ah, linger on, thou art so fair!" The character of a life within this framework is yet to be determined, and in its discovery Faust tries out and rejects the major alternative paths of life.

The life of unceasing making to which he is pointed calls for a renewal of his vital impulses in dionysian waters. The Devil opens these seas to Faust, hoping to drown him in them; Faust seeks in them only nourishment for his own development. The coarser release of primitive impulses in Auerbach's Cellar, the Witch's Kitchen, and the Dionysian festival of the Walpurgis Night do not give this nourishment. His love for Margaret, tragic though it is, does. To Margaret this love has the purity, the depth, the detachment of ideal Christian love. To Faust it is, on the surface, the desire to drink of life in the passionate possession of a woman; it is not something in which his life of action can rest. Thoughtless in his treatment of her, inconsiderate in the indulgence of his passion, led by the Devil to the unwitting killing of her mother and her brother, responsible for the death of Margaret herself and of her child, Faust leaves Margaret and the path of Christian love to follow the Devil into the wider world. Margaret shudders at Faust for this alliance; but true to the Christian ideal she represents, she does not seek to retain him: desperate though she is, yet, aware of his fate, she frees him with the words, "No, you must stay alive, you must indeed!" That Faust has found in his love for Margaret, a love genuine at the core, the source for the purification of his promethean strivings, only later becomes evident.

Faust enters the wider world of human society. In the life of the emperor's court he encounters the easygoing pleasure seeking of people in power unscrupulous in the use of means to attain more power. Faust links himself with these persons in order to obtain means for carrying out his own ideals; but while this linkage with "Mohammedan" forces is made possible through his own possessiveness and willingness to use the forces of

magic to achieve his ends, it leads Faust into slaughter and
destruction:

> To kindle life's fair torch we did aspire
> And seas of flame—and what a flame!—embrace us!

Faust has the constant dionysian need to align himself with
the cosmic sources of creativity. Before the entrance into the
emperor's services, he seeks—again by the help of Mephistopheles—access to the Mothers, symbols of the forces and activities out of which the existing world springs. The Devil—
the irreligious one, with no fixed point of attachment but with
the demonic restlessness necessary for creation—hopes that
Faust will lose himself in contact with this realm of "formation, transformation, Eternal Mind's eternal re-creation," a
realm which to the Devil is a void and its products worthless
because of their transiency: "Of what avail's perpetual creation,
If later swept off to annihilation?" Faust, unlike the dionysian
mystic, does not turn to the eternal play of the universe to lose
himself; he seeks the sources of creativity: "That art and power
I may there augment."

Strengthened in this contact, Faust turns to the classical
Apollonian world of beauty, symbolized in Helen. Out of union
with Helen, Euphorion is born; his death in frantic flight is a
symbol of the inadequacy of a merely poetic or imaginative
version of Prometheanism such as the Renaissance and Byron
seem to have meant to Goethe. And though Helen herself dies,
her robes, transformed into clouds, carry Faust into the air;
something has been gained by the Promethean through contact
with the world of Apollo:

> Let not the garment go. . . . .
> . . . . Make use of the high
> And priceless boon, and rising soar aloft.

> Swift over all things common will it bear thee
> Away through ether while thou canst endure.

By the end of the drama, Faust, now an old man, has clarified the goal of his life search, and the Promethean path, dis-
entangled from its rivals and its own corruptions, stands forth.
Magic has been spurned, dionysian sensualism and mysticism
are left behind, possessiveness and the use of blind force to
achieve human ends are relinquished. There remains man,
standing before nature, united with fellow men in co-operative
endeavor, utilizing his human energies, his technologies, and
his mind in a process of continually transforming his corporate
life in the face of the cosmic powers which threaten its dissolution. Faust, though blinded by care, is at work on a project
to dam back the sea, and his final words before he dies are
Promethean words:

> Thus space to many millions I will give
> Where, though not safe, yet free and active they may live.
> Green fertile fields where straightway from their birth
> Both men and beast live happy on the newest earth,
> Settled forthwith along the mighty hill
> Raised by a daring, busy people's will.
> Within, a land like Paradise; outside,
> Up to the brink may rage the mighty tide,
> And where it gnaws and would burst through or sap,
> A common impulse hastes to close the gap.
> Yes! to this thought I hold unswerving,
> To wisdom's final fruit, profoundly true:
> Of freedom and of life he only is deserving
> Who every day must conquer them anew.
> Thus here, by danger girt, the active day
> Of childhood, manhood, age will pass away.
> Aye, such a throng I fain would see,

Stand on free soil among a people free.
Then might I say, that moment seeing:
"Ah, linger on, thou art so fair!"
The traces of my earthly being
Can perish not in aeons—they are there!
That lofty moment I now feel in this:
I now enjoy the highest moment's bliss.

The final pages of the drama serve to make clear Goethe's conviction that the Promethean activity of unceasing making must be purified by the forces represented in Margaret's love and generalized in love to mankind. Faust after death has still an evolution to undergo. Whether the detachment involved in Christian love and in art and in science, and the giving of the dionysian forces their due for what they helped effect, would lead Faust to a more inclusive view than that of the Promethean is another question; in the Faust as finally presented to us we have the literary symbol of man the Promethean maker. Mephistopheles says of him:

> Him could no pleasure sate, suffice no bliss,
> So wooed he ever changeful phantoms' favour.

John Dewey has given the Promethean attitude its most generalized formulation and its widest application: he has built a religious way of life around this attitude, and he has implemented it with a Promethean interpretation of philosophy, science, art, morality, and democracy. His writings, as the apologetics of the Promethean religion, mark a decisive moment in the history of Western culture, and in the history of the United States in particular. In them the aspirations and heritage of the Enlightenment and of nineteenth century British liberalism are preserved and purified, and focused with the resources of the twentieth century upon its present cultural crisis. It is true that Dewey himself is the heir of the development of American pragmatism attained through the efforts of Peirce and James and Mead; it is also true that Dewey's later writings show indications of the Maitreyan type of man. And yet the net result of his long labors is to hold before us, at this moment of Promethean man's ordeal, the image of this man; and his endeavor is to strengthen the wavering faith of this man in himself and our faith in him. Dewey is the clearest philosophic voice of Prometheus, and it is as such that we will envisage him.

It is natural that a Promethean philosophy as found in Dewey should appear in the New World, for in traveling to these shores Prometheus had temporarily left behind a culture which curtailed his activities; engaged in building a new culture, confident of his energies and his intelligence, and needing all the help he could gain by the techniques made available by science, his aspirations could more easily seek verbal formulation, and without the overtones of repression and suffering that his presence in an older culture always called forth. As the culmination of the Promethean America that has been, and the prophet of the Promethean America that might yet be, Dewey's work is of high significance.

Dewey has preferred to call his version of pragmatism by the name of instrumentalism. The focus of his vision is, in a large sense of the term, technological; it has been directed upon the agencies which men have developed for the more adequate satisfaction and co-ordination of their desires—desires molded, amplified, specified in the complex society of the modern world, and agencies made possible by the co-operative endeavors of men and women within this world. His outlook—to use a term he has recently employed—is that of cultural naturalism: he sees men as natural biological entities whose life processes are continuous with the processes of physical nature but transformed radically through participation in communal life.

The account of human nature which was given in an earlier chapter is essentially Deweyan, except for the fact that Dewey has stressed primarily the transformations which all men undergo through participation in society and the resulting transformation of society which such men in turn do and can effect; he has not been concerned—as was James—with the differences of types of personality. And this exception is of importance. Dewey has, it is true, transcended the rank opposition of individual and society, and such transcendence is one of the key achievements of the pragmatic movement. If he sees individuals in terms of their social setting, he is equally aware of the fact that societies have no existence over and above interrelated individuals: he consistently envisages the individual as "the reconstructive center of society." If he is demanding a society which prepares the conditions for the appearance of individuals capable of intelligent self-direction and initiative, he is also demanding a socially oriented individual who uses his own unique (though socially derived) resources for the continual reconstruction of the society in which he lives. The result is that Dewey is predominantly attentive to those features of the human personality which "man as man" owes to participation in complex social interactions; it is in this sense that his view is essentially social. He thinks of mind, of morality, of art, of philosophy, of religion in essentially social terms; his eye is everywhere upon the common values which men share in virtue of communal life and those features of individual activities which support and enhance such common values; his very lack of consideration of individual differences is the reflex of his almost exclusive concern for those promethean activities of individuals in which physical and social processes are transformed in the service of values which men share or may share in common. The net result is that, almost unconsciously, Promethean man is given a preferred status. The Deweyan ideal man is socialized Promethean man: he is man living outwardly in society and environing nature, utilizing his emotions, his intelligence, and his activity to transform this society and this nature so that the values of society (and of himself as a social being) are progressively satisfied, enlarged, and co-ordinated. To effect the socialization, moralization, of Promethean man, and to put at his disposal all the agencies of an advanced culture: this is the key to Dewey's lifework. And in this work Dewey has revealed his own Promethean nature: as a Promethean moralist and religionist his activities have everywhere tended to restrain the dionysian and buddhistic factors of human nature in so far as they weakened the socially reconstructive orientation of the individual, and to harness whenever possible these factors into furthering the Promethean campaign. He has likewise opposed any version of supernaturalism which tended to drain off human energies from their naturalistic utilization. He has brought to the forefront the Promethean facet of philosophy, art, and science. He has formulated "the deepest problem of modern life" as "the problem of restoring integration and co-operation between man's beliefs about the world in which he lives and his beliefs about the values and purposes that should direct his conduct"; and to this problem he has given a Promethean answer: man by the use of his scientific intelligence and its dependent technology can reconstruct his cultural and social life by the very agencies of science and technology which disintegrated his earlier forms of social life. In freeing the Promethean attitude for a continual remaking of human life,

Dewey elevates this attitude into a chosen path of life—into a Promethean religion.

It is a common insistence of thinkers such as Nietzsche and Marx that philosophy is not simply a scientific enterprise, but has the responsibility for transvaluing values and changing the world. Dewey too thinks of philosophy as performing at all times, though in varying ways, a socially directive function: that of defining "the larger patterns of continuity which are woven in effecting the enduring junctions of a stubborn past and an insistent future." The stubborn past is to him the gap which has grown up in Western culture between its inherited moral and religious ideals and the ideas and practices developed out of science and technology; the insistent future is the imperative need of reintegrating ideals and ideas, precepts and practices.

Dewey stresses continuity, and while his answer accepts Prometheus, it incorporates certain features of the Christian moral heritage. Prometheus is in this way moralized; his reconstructive activities are guided by a generalized love for human life itself. Dewey sides with science and technology; at this point he allows no retreat. Human ideals are to be implemented by these agencies; Prometheus is to go farther forward on his path; his difficulties arise through not having completed his task: "The great scientific revolution is still to come. . . . Science has hardly begun to modify men's fundamental acts and attitudes in social relations." It is to the carrying out of this continuation of the Promethean revolution that Dewey summons contemporary Promethean man.

The major instrument—the tool of tools—which man has at

his command is thought to be the scientific habit of mind. Mind in all its forms is itself conceived naturalistically, instrumentally, socially. Its roots lie in the unintended indications which one animal gives to another of the action appropriate in a common situation, as when the quack of the female duck orients the young to some feature of the environment which threatens the security of the family group; its fruits appear in the complex linguistic processes in which men deliberately utilize the resources of each other for the effectuation of their individual and social purposes. In this perspective there is no sharp difference in kind between mind and body, or between the spiritual and the material. Mentality arises in a complex functional relation between organisms and their physical and social environments in which certain features of the world serve as clues for taking account of other features of the world relevant to existing purposes. The minded organism is no disembodied spectator of the world, but a being threading his way through a world which provides both obstacles and supports, by means of the forethought which the socially conditioned linguistic processes make possible.

Dewey regards science as the most effective form of intelligence which man has attained. Through its co-operative activity it provides the most accurate and the most general statements of what will be encountered if actions of various sorts are undertaken. Its objectivity is a social objectivity; its detachment is the clear eye of more comprehensive attachments. The scientific mentality is conceived to be the supreme agency for the realization and progressive modification of human life. It is as a rational cultural animal that man becomes an agent in the control of his destiny, and stands before an open future whose lineaments he may to an unknown degree help to shape.

Intelligence is, on this approach, placed in the context of

human activity; it is conceived to arise out of the problems which such activity encounters, to be itself a form of (symbolically directed) activity, and to find its test and its significance in the reconstruction of activity which it makes possible. It has been a task—indeed, the central task—of Dewey's technical writings to defend this view of mind and to show that the operations of scientific intelligence are not restricted to the study of physical nature but can be extended to all of the problems which beset individual and social life. This has meant that he has had to make evident an essential continuity between the scientific process of making statements about the world and the process of approval and disapproval characteristic of aesthetic, moral, and political evaluations; and in showing this continuity he has made available for man's cultural problems the method of intelligence which has been so successful in dealing with physical nature.

So close is the relation of thought and interest on this naturalistic theory that reason is not to be conceived as merely supplying an external agency by which existing desires seek satisfaction: the hints which forethought supplies as to the consequences of possible modes of action affect the impulses themselves that would issue, if unchecked, in these actions. The use of the instrument modifies the purposes for which it was invoked; the means available progressively modify the ends sought; man as a system of interests changes his interests in the reflective activities embarked upon to satisfy them. There is then no static set of values to which human life is committed: the interests which surround and direct some phase of reflection may themselves be evaluated by reflection within some other operating system of interests. It is a particular situation with particular problems encountered by specific interests which initiates and terminates each instance of reflection. And, if Dewey is right, there is no situation, no means, no end, not open to intelligent control by being made the object of reflective attention.

Dewey conceives the dilemma of modern man as having arisen out of the impact of science and technology on his inherited culture. He finds the way out of this dilemma to lie in the solution of particular problems by the further extension of the method of scientific intelligence—and not in appeals to class or to race, not in withdrawing to an individual island of contemplative salvation, not in submerging reason in action under a tidal wave of dionysian abandon. Promethean man is to build a new culture by the very agencies which have unsettled the old culture. Thus is continuity to be made between the stubborn past and the insistent future, and Prometheus unbound.

Dewey's Promethean orientation is most evident in his treatment of morality. What he does in effect is to accept the emphasis upon the unique development of each individual (a consistent though rare development of the Christian attitude of love), but to put at the service of this attitude the armory of the Promethean technologist. Insensibly, almost imperceptibly, the traditional morality is transformed into a Promethean morality, and the Promethean is, in the same process, moralized. Morality itself becomes a phase of the reconstructive activity of the Promethean when this is applied to particular situations in which the interest systems of individuals come into conflict. The Promethean simply extends to the sphere of social relations his characteristic mode of activity.

This development had been going on for some time—in J. S. Mill and the English utilitarians; in William James among the pragmatists. James, for instance, in his essay on "The Moral Philosopher and the Moral Life," had stated:

> There is but one unconditional commandment, which is to seek incessantly, with fear and trembling, so to vote and to act as to bring about the very largest total universe of good which we can see. . . . Every real dilemma is in literal strictness a unique situation, and the exact combination of ideals realized and ideals disappointed which each decision creates is always a universe without precedent, and for which no previous rule exists.

In conformity with this position James had given "the guiding principle for ethical philosophy . . . to satisfy as many demands as we can." And that this maxim requires resourceful inventiveness, and not merely the admission of existing interests, is brought out by his injunction: "*Invent* some manner of realizing your own ideals which will also satisfy the alien demands." Mead, too, at a later time stressed the view that moral action requires "such a reconstruction of the situation that different and enlarged and more adequate personalities may emerge." Dewey's version of morality is a systematization of this general theme, with emphasis upon the situational context of moral action, upon the similarity of the moral judgment to the scientific hypothesis, and upon the actual transformation of the social situation which moral activity involves.

On this reinterpretation, morality itself is an instrument, a technology, to be used in so far as it meets its specific purpose and to be changed as that purpose can be better served. Since the Deweyan moralist spurns no interest as such and no technique by which interests can be satisfied, the moral goal becomes one of so reconstructing specific situations that the maximum satisfaction of all conflicting interests can be attained. Moral reflection becomes simply a special case of reflection: it is directed to a social situation in which interests conflict, and it functions as an instrument in meeting the problems posed by the specific situation. If it is guided by love, in that the interests of all the persons involved are respected and have a voice in determining what is to be done, it must also be guided by the best knowledge available as to what the actual interests are and what techniques are efficacious in satisfying them. It is true that past moral injunctions represent the accumulated experience of man in meeting just such problems, and are to be given due weight; but they now function as hypotheses and not as dogmas to be blindly followed. The specific situation becomes the matrix which sets the problem and tests the answer; as interests, knowledge, and techniques change, moral action takes on an ever-new form. The opposition between morality, science, and technology is in this way negated. A belief as to what in a specific case is morally right can only be tested experimentally by acting on the hypothesis and noting whether it performs in this case the function guiding moral reflection: namely, the reconstruction of the world such that the problem involved in a particular conflict of interests is resolved.

Not only is morality on this interpretation assimilated to the Promethean outlook; the position inevitably involves a preference for the Promethean type of person. At first sight this is not evident, for it would seem as though the moral person would simply take into account whatever types of persons he in fact encountered, and attempt to deal with the peculiarity of their demands as well as possible. No doubt this is, formally, involved in Dewey's position—for insensitivity to individual differences would in fact be an admission of failure to do justice to the specific interests operative in a specific situation. And yet the moral motivation of Dewey's whole philosophy involves inherently the desire to have as many persons as possible morally active (in the sense defined by this view of morality). This means that these persons will, at least in this one area of their lives, be Prometheans; the temper of Dewey's whole educational system and the impact of his writings is, accordingly, to set the seal of approval upon Promethean man. The Promethean needs converts, for the technology which he accepts is socially sustained and dependent upon co-operation. And a morality which is a phase of such technology will need wide co-operation; its advocates inevitably will train men in their image.

Prometheus turned moralist becomes in his moral life what he is in the rest of his life: a maker, an inventor, an experimenter, engaged in the continual co-operative reconstruction of the world in which he operates.

Art is also drawn by Dewey into the agencies of Promethean man. The whole tenor of his important work, *Art as Experience*, is to oppose the conception of art as "the beauty parlor of civilization." As against views which make of art an esoteric and isolated domain, Dewey stresses the continuity of art with normal experience, its function of developing and accentuating "what is characteristically valuable in things of every day enjoyment," its linkage of the intellectual, emotional, and sensuous aspects of experience, its role as a form of communication in extending the range of socially shared values, its contribution to man's task of improving his environment, its educational influence in the integration of the self, its contribution to man's moral endeavors. His view breaks down the isolation of the fine and applied arts, the pseudo-opposition of the "emotional" "unthinking" artist to the reflecting experimental scientist, the cloistering of the arts from the impact of an industrial and technological world. There is no narrow utilitarianism in this view, but its net result is to restore to art its continuity with the rest of human life, and to see its function within this context.

To say that life has interests or that it seeks values is to state the same situation from the side of the impulse and from the side of what would satisfy the impulse. The pursuit of values is aided by whatever presents vividly the values in question and in a form in which the separate values sustain and amplify each other: art is the agency for such presentation of value. The artist thinks and works in a medium, and is to that degree a maker, a technologist; in so far as the medium is handled in such a way that the values to which the artist is attentive are perceived in the object he makes, the artist has in fact remade the world nearer to human desire. To this degree the aesthetic experience is a finality, a consummation, a victory. But since the values with which the artist deals are not in the main unique values of the medium alone, and are not exhausted in their aesthetic presentation, art is also a means: an agency by which men bring to consciousness their values and goals, attain greater clarity and consistency in what they seek, and obtain stimulation in the arduous and never-ending task of remaking themselves and the physical-social world in which they dwell.

Art in this way becomes a phase of Promethean activity, and an agency which supports the other agencies which man has elaborated. It has its own unique function to perform, and its importance is in no way diminished by, or in opposition to, the importance of science and the machines it spawns. Few philosophers, indeed, have given to art a higher place in human life. In seeing the mutually supporting place of art, science, and the ordinary forms of technology, and in demanding of art that it suffuse the whole of modern life with its conjoint blessings of consummation, communication, and intensification, Dewey has opened to contemporary art a wide perspective and a high opportunity. He has justified its direction, and aided the further release of its energies.

Art, Dewey has noted, is often "more moral than moralities." For the traditional morality constantly tends to become formal and insensitive to the actual values and conflicts of living persons. The artist, like the scientist, is "on the growing edge of things," alert to the novel, the insistent, the forming. He too is an experimenter, snaring in a medium the significance he apprehends, molding an object in which he and others can perceive and receive the significance he has been able to impart to some segment of life. There are no works of art absolute in their achievements and normative for all aesthetic creation; the problems of art are as novel and variegated as the changing forms of human desire; art is a phase of the continual remaking by men of their world and themselves.

Dewey has at once caught the Promethean facet of art, and enlarged the Promethean vision in bringing art within the range of Promethean activity.

In an early paper on the *Ethics of Democracy*, Dewey characterized democracy "as a social, that is to say, an ethical conception"; and he added, "upon its ethical significance is based its significance as governmental"—today he would undoubtedly add "and as economical." If we keep in mind Dewey's interpretation of morality, his conception of democracy can best be stated as that form of society which adopts the method of morality for the solution of its problems. A democratic society —to use a phrase of George Mead—has institutionalized revolution. It has committed itself to the use of agencies by which the clash of interests of its members can be given a moral resolution. It must give to each of its members "a chance . . . to become a person" so that every member, to the limit of his ability, partakes in the continual remaking of the common life. It must utilize to the full the scientific habit of mind in effecting its continual transition. It must ever transform its educational, political, and economic institutions to the end that its citizens attain an ever fuller development of their potentialities. A democratic society, on this moral interpretation, has no commitments beyond a concern that each individual be fitted to play his part in building the society in which he lives, and a devotion to the method of morality by which changes in the individual and society are to be effected.

The respect for the development of each individual establishes a link between Dewey and the Christian heritage, but the novel note is the utilization of the technological agencies of society to implement and realize the naturalistically conceived goal of morality. The attempt to give each individual a creative role in society requires that he be furnished access to all the agencies of the moral life: his capacity for independent reflection must be developed; his allegiance to the interests of his fellow men and the social whole must be cultivated; he must be supplied with the most accurate knowledge available; he must command the best techniques at hand; he must have the economic resources to give him the security and the leisure necessary for effective participation in the cultural life of the community.

These points had long been stressed by Dewey and are the keystones of his educational policies; the last point—the economic transformation which the further evolution of democracy is felt to involve—has in recent years been in the forefront

of his attention. He is in effect asking Promethean man to transform the economic basis of society so that Promethean activity
in wider cultural domains be released where it is now dammed.
"Socialized economy," he writes in *Liberalism and Social Action*, "is the means of free individual development as the
end. . . . The only form of enduring social organization that
is now possible is one in which the new forces of productivity
are cooperatively controlled and used in the interest of the effective liberty and the cultural development of the individuals
that constitute society." Such an economic democracy, supple-
menting political democracy, is regarded by Dewey as the next
step in the realization of moral democracy. That he regards
it as the locus of immediate activity is clear; that it is a means
to a moral end is equally clear: "The economic-material phase
of life, which belongs in the basal ganglia of society, has
usurped for more than a century the cortex of the social body."
It is through the democratic control of this phase of life that
its usurpation of the social cortex is to be ended and new democratic vistas opened.

Democracy becomes a social way of life, a method and an
attitude rather than a set of dogmas. This stress on method
is so central to Dewey's attitude that it must be singled out for
emphasis. It is analogous to the reliance in science upon a self-
corrective method rather than upon the doctrines which the
use of this method has at any given time produced. Conceiving
of democracy as a method of social action has important consequences. It is a two-edged weapon, directed both against those
who identify a democratic society with any existing set of political and economic institutions, and against those who counsel
the use of nondemocratic means to achieve professedly democratic ends; with the Promethean sword of "democracy as
method" Dewey has simultaneously attacked the Apollonians

who fear the further transformation of a democratic society, and the Fascist and Communist totalitarians (the "Mohammedans") who endanger the very continuance of a democratic society in the means they invoke for its presumed defense. To oppose the conservatives, Dewey summons the Prometheans to attack the economic bottleneck; to oppose the totalitarians, Dewey urges the Prometheans to hold fast to democratic means compatible with the democratic end of "free individual development." Conservatives, Fascists, and Communists alike seem to him to stop the line of moral advance; against them he summons a Promethean America to a "renascent liberalism," to the ideal of a moral democracy implicit in its history.

A democratic society, as Dewey (and Mead) have conceived it, is an open society, continually creating itself anew in terms of the expanding and varying interests of its members through the use of a morally controlled intelligence and technology. Such a society is a Promethean society erected upon a Promethean morality.

In *A Common Faith* Dewey has given the final elaboration to his position in showing that the attitude he has championed is religious in quality. This leads him to an interpretation of religion in general as a background for the view that the aspirations of modern men, when freed from the historic religions, still furnish the basis for a new religiosity. At first sight it would not seem just to Dewey himself to speak of his "religion." For his whole argument proceeds by attributing to a religion specific creeds and institutions, and by regarding "religiousness" as an attitude which requires no such creeds and institutions; his book is in this respect an attempt to free the religious attitude from religions: "I am not proposing a religion, but rather the emancipation of elements and outlooks that may be called religious." Nevertheless, since we have stressed the relation of religion to a way of life, in terms we have been using Dewey's writings may be regarded as the apologetics of Promethean religion; and his distinction between a religion and a religious attitude may be interpreted as his way of stressing the fact that a Promethean religion, by its very nature, can be committed to no dogmas and institutions which stand in the way of its own dogma and institution: growth and the agencies which make for growth. Commitments are no less commitments because they are not supernaturally directed, and methods which permit and direct change are not necessarily less institutionalized than those which aim to eternalize whatever already is.

Dewey interprets a religious attitude as a general attitude by which the self, with its ideals, and the environing world are brought into active interaction and mutual support. In contrast to particular adjustments to particular situations,

There are also changes in ourselves in relation to the world in which we live that are much more inclusive and deep-seated. They relate not to this and that want in relation to this and that condition of our surroundings, but pertain to our being in its entirety. Because of their scope, this modification of ourselves is enduring. It lasts through any amount of vicissitude of circumstances, internal and external. There is a composing and harmonizing of the various elements of our being such that, in spite of the changes in the special conditions which surround us, these conditions are also arranged, settled, in relation to us. . . . Whenever this change takes place there is a definitely religious attitude.

In the development of this approach to the religious attitude,

Dewey shows that the unification of the self which such an attitude expresses always involves ideal factors: the self "gives its allegiance to inclusive ideal ends" and links its forces with those forces in the imaginatively conceived universe which promise support. He suggests that the term 'god' designates the "*active* relation between ideal and actual"; in the concrete, at a given time and place, the meaning of the term would vary with "the ideal ends that . . . one acknowledges as having authority over his volition and emotion, the values to which one is supremely devoted, as far as these ends, through imagination, take on unity." In so far as these ideal ends differ, the relation of individuals to the universe differs, and their religious attitudes differ. Dewey has in this way freed the religious attitude to seek new forms.

The attitude which has directed his own life, and which his writings encourage as an attitude appropriate for this human epoch, is unmistakable: his own ideal is one for which "growth is a higher value and ideal than is sheer attainment," for which "a socialized economy" is the basis for "free individual development," and for which natural processes discerned and guided by scientific intelligence provide the technological means. This is the attitude of Prometheanism freed from supernatural moorings, amplified by a congenial interpretation of art and morality and democracy, armored by the scientific attitude and the resources of modern technology, and elevated to religious rank.

The emphasis that has been put upon intelligence as a method should not mislead anyone. Intelligence, as distinct from the older conception of reason, is inherently involved in action. Moreover, there is no opposition between it and emotion. There is such a thing as passionate intelligence, as ardor in behalf of light shining into the murky places of social existence, and as zeal for its refreshing and purifying effect. The whole story of man shows that there are no objects that may not deeply stir engrossing emotion. One of the few experiments in the attachment of emotion to ends that mankind has not tried is that of devotion, so intense as to be religious, to intelligence as a force in social action.

James remarked in one of his letters that "as life closes, all a man has done seems like one cry or sentence"; Dewey's long life has been one cry to modern man for "devotion, so intense as to be religious, to intelligence as a force in social action."

The Promethean personality is primarily promethean (so-matotonic), secondarily dionysian, and least of all buddhistic. The Promethean is a self that has transformed itself into activity. This activity is inherently restless: it cannot remain anchored in any of its products; it can only ask "What more can I do?" If it links itself with some doctrine of immortality—as it has often done—it is only to envisage a never-ending life of the same activity it manifests here. Its activity pulls it away from Dionysian enjoyment and Buddhistic contemplation alike; to persons strongly dionysian it seems a shallow, unaesthetic orientation, lacking the note of the festival and the delirium of abandonment to the instant; to persons strongly buddhistic the Promethean seems a restless uncentered slave to time's pressure. The conservatives at all times look upon the Promethean as an innovator unsettling all the stability that men have attained. It is not surprising that the notes of loneliness and suffering have been blended with his name, and that he has fought under any banner which might supply him with an outlet for his energies.

The Promethean is often a Don Quixote of the ideal; his

own allegiance is to ideals in the plural, whatever their source. Give him an interest to serve and his fingers seek for the material to satisfy it. He has fought alike under the banner of the Holy Grail and the modern munition makers; he has sold his services in turn to Christians, Apollonians, Mohammedans. When one army falls, he is likely to join the survivors. He may follow blindly those who promise to use his activity, even though the result is in the end the shackling of this very activity. Rarely does he, as in the case of Dewey, see that the process of continual reconstruction is the supreme ideal to which he must in consistency remain devoted.

The strength and weakness of the Promethean attitude are objectively underlined in the civilization of the predominantly Promethean West. There is an heroic note in this civilization. It has taken the fire from the gods, and it has eaten of the tree of knowledge to storm the tree of life. Against the wrath of Zeus and the expulsion from the Garden of Eden, it has dared to build, and ever rebuild, a human citadel in which man consciously takes control of his own future. It has met thunderbolts and curses with reason and art and technology. It has looked fearlessly into the faces of the gods and sought their genealogies; its vision has expanded to take in the vast spaces of the stars and has contracted to make visible minute living entities and nonliving processes; it has challenged death and suffering as foes to be met and not as friends to be embraced; it has ransacked the earth for the elements of its making and remade them into new instruments and new habitations; it has dared of late to look into itself and to bring itself into the sphere of its own making.

And yet this civilization has paid the price of its zeal. Its pride has often become conceit; it has a provincial attitude to other cultures; it is often intolerant of other types of personality;

in moments of victory it has shown a superficial optimism; in moments of defeat it has sought refuge in histrionic defiance. The aspects of human nature that it has neglected have sought their revenge. The buddhistic and dionysian elements in Christianity have never been far under the surface, and periodically erupt. Always a Blake or a Rousseau or a Tolstoy or a Nietzsche is at hand to laugh the existing technologically supported social structure to scorn. The Apollonian is always anxious to stop the process of continual remaking at the level it has reached. The Mohammedan is ever ready to turn the Promethean's inventiveness to his own ends. Waves of romanticism and the dionysianism of power rush in at the least break in the sea wall, and the breaks are now visible to every eye. The artists have mercilessly depicted the wounds in this culture, and have often turned away to their own retreats. The thinker, like the artist, constantly has yearned to become a spectator: to crucify himself that a purity of vision uncontaminated by the needs of action be regained. In science, in art, in asceticism, the Promethean West has disclosed its unsatisfied desire for detachment. It has even more markedly disclosed its dionysian cravings: the old Mysteries have run a subterranean course under the visible façade; no civilization has tried so hard to exhaust the resources of sentimental and passionate love; recurrent gigantic wars have released impulses which stable society has repressed; the restraints of the social self are periodically dissolved in alcohol. The burden of Prometheus has been a heavy one. Yet his will has remained unbroken. And his forces are still not spent.

Dewey has clarified the Promethean's vision, and opened for him new spheres of activity in the remaking of human life. In calling him back to his own ideal of never-ending reconstruction, he has helped to free him from service to seductive ideals essentially alien to his own activity. But Dewey has, at the same time, inevitably if unconsciously, tempered the Promethean's ardor: for the call to art and to science will show him not merely the promethean side of these activities but will fashion his eye for the enjoyment of the present and free his mind to some degree from the practical urgencies of the present; and the moralization of the Promethean will uncover for him forms of love and companionship to which he has been insensitive. Dewey points beyond Promethean man as Nietzsche pierced the mantle of the god Dionysus, and as Buddhism overflowed its first formulation. Beyond these banners there is the Maitreyan banner; there perhaps is the rallying ground for frustrated Prometheans and a bewildered Promethean West.

VI. Apollo, Christ, and Mohammed

"The mean state is in all things praiseworthy."

Aristotle:
Nicomachean Ethics

"And one of the scribes came . . . and asked him,
Which is the first commandment of all? And Jesus answered him; The first of all the commandments is, Hear,
O Israel; the Lord our God is one Lord; and thou shalt
love the Lord thy God with all thy heart, and with all thy
soul, and with all thy mind, and with all thy strength.
And the second is like, namely this, Thou shalt love thy
neighbour as thyself. There is none other commandment
greater than these."

Mark 12:28-31

"He it is who sent His Apostle with guidance and the religion of truth to set it above all religion; averse although
the idolaters may be.
"O ye who believe! shall I lead you to a merchandise
which will save you from grievous woe?
"To believe in God and His Apostle, and to fight strenu-
ously in God's cause with your property and your persons;
that is better for you if ye did but know!
"He will pardon you your sins, and bring you into gardens beneath which rivers flow, and goodly dwellings in
gardens of Eden;—that is the mighty bliss!
"And other things which ye love,—help from God and
victory nigh! so do thou give the glad tidings unto the
believers!"

The Koran

VI

Apollo, Christ, and Mohammed

WE NOW turn to a consideration of the Apollonian, Christian, and Mohammedan paths of life. These paths are more familiar than those so far considered: the fact that all three of them seek salvation within the framework of a social community links them together more intimately than is possible for the more individualistic Buddhist, Dionysian, and Promethean paths, and insures that all members of society will hear their voices through the institutionalized organs of social control. For this reason, among others, these three paths will be treated in less detail, and their critique will be more cursory. As paths of life, however, they are in every way co-ordinate with those which have already passed before us.

There is in many eyes something frantic, forced, colossal in the Buddhist regime to control the unruly self, in the Dionysian liberation of the self from the agencies within and without which seek to control it, and in the Promethean restlessness ever to be making the world anew; when we pause before the shrine of Apollo we experience a calmness, a release of tension, a mood of acceptance which no other of the great gods permits. For Apollo was the bright god, the genial god, the god of the high noon. His festivals were daytime festivals—not celebrated in winter or at night or in secrecy. Harmony, moderation, clarity are his characteristics; he is no friend of sorrow or solitude, death is banished from his presence, and excess withers. His figure meets us everywhere in the middle period

of Greek civilization, so much so that the West has tended
to identify Greek culture with Apollo. And though such identification is an undue simplification, facilitated by the accidents
which determined what should survive of the Greek culture in
the culture which displaced it, it remains true that much of
Greek art, literature, architecture, science, and philosophy ex-
plains why the Western mind has come to envisage the classical
under the form of Apollo, and to seek with nostalgia at his
shrine for an antidote to its own gargantuan restlessness.

Apollo was the god of the higher social life which had attained orderliness without sterility, contemplation without inaction, integration without the suppression of multifariousness.
He was the protector of the high achievements which men had
attained; like Vishnu in the Hindu trinity, he was the conserver
of such attainments against the new forms of existence which
ever flow from the promethean Brahma and from the tendencies
to dissolution ever involved in the dionysian Siva. The oracular
utterances of Apollo did not lead to innovations: they conse-
crated the forms of art and morality and society which had
already become socially approved. When the voice of Dionysus
became ever more insistent in Greece, Apollo—as Nietzsche
discerned—threw his mantle over this insurgent life and attempted to give it restraint within the forms of Apollonian
art and cult practices. Pindar remarks in the fifth Pythian ode
that Apollo "brings into our hearts the peaceful law-abiding
temper."

Under the guidance of Apollo we respect the forms of life
which men have so painfully acquired. In the deepest sense of
the word, Apollo is a conserving deity, holding in check the
forces of renewal and disintegration, turning the individual
outward to participate in the established social life of the
community, seducing his devotees with the imaged significance

which this communal life has already achieved, approving stability and moderation, and threatening the individual who
strains at the social leash with the punishments which gods and
men mete out to those who transgress the just limits set by man
and cosmos. Greek tragedy is pervaded by the sense of a social
and cosmic order which it is fatal to transgress; if Sophocles
reflects best this Apollonian motive, it is nevertheless true that
the more promethean characters in Aeschylus and the more
dionysian ones of Euripides, while in a sense approved, owe
their tragic state precisely to those traits of character which
cause them to deviate from the norm of moderation under
which the Apollonian looks at himself, his society, and his
universe.

The follower of Apollo is, then, an active socially oriented
individual, capable of energetic participation in the established
cultural forms of his community, but apprehensive of deviation
from these forms; his preference is for stability rather than
change ("being" rather than "becoming"); he seeks moderation in his feelings and actions and thoughts; he is ill at ease
in the presence of any emotion, or deed, or thought, which
seems to him "excessive"; his aim is self-controlled realization
of himself in a stable society; his gaze is on the specific, the well-
formed, the finite, the clear, the near; he shuns night, sorrow,
solitude, death, frenzy, immensity; his life is lived in the day-
light of society.

Aristotle's writings are the Canon of the Apollonian personality. They are the record of a son of Apollo living in the after-
glow of the Periclean age in which such personalities had for
the moment come to dominance. Aristotle is no exception to the

principle that the formulator and defender of a way of life is more intellectual, more "buddhistic" than the mode of life formulated and defended; and though this is reflected in his own writings, it does not blur the fact that the preferred type of man which stands back of and shines through the Aristotelian corpus is Apollonian man.

Aristotle's concern is encyclopedic: he follows with a generous and approving eye the science, the literature, the forms of society dominant in his day; he wishes to understand, to classify, to systematize this cultural heritage; the spirit is not one of reform or innovation, but a conservation of this heritage by exhibiting its essential nature and the factors making for deviation from the norms already established. The whole of his philosophy is in effect a justification of these Apollonian norms by giving them a cosmic support "in the nature of things." The world as seen by such eyes is an arena in which the same forms ("essences," "essential natures," "species") ever struggle to embody themselves in actuality and to hold on to this embodiment against the forces which make for change. There is no beginning to the world process, no end, no general straining toward a far-off distant goal—only an ever orderly process in which a fixed number of patterns manifest themselves under favorable conditions and momentarily lose their hold on actuality under unfavorable conditions. Characteristically Apollonian is the belief that these fixed and essential natures are already realized and discernible in the present; one needs only to be sufficiently discriminating and painstaking to see in the present what each kind of thing, and what the whole of things, is. It is as though the universe graciously had presented itself completely to the man of Periclean Greece for his understanding, his delight, and his guidance. Here, for a moment, the nature of things was disclosed and human life consummated; if change was to come it would be a change from the norm and "to the bad," and could be ignored, with the confidence that in time what was fit, orderly, harmonious, "good" would again appear.

The issues can be brought to a focus by a glance at the way of life expressed and defended in Aristotle's *Nicomachean Ethics*—the handbook of the Apollonian. It is characteristic of this book—and of most treatises on ethics—that the preference for a certain type of man is disguised under a presumably "objective" analysis of human nature, of "man as man." Man's essential nature is "rational"; and since the happiness of each being is to live according to its nature, man's task is to interpenetrate and direct his activities as a doer, a maker, and a knower by his distinguishing and characteristic faculty of rational self-control. He will as a matter of course live his life in society, but his goal will be the harmony, the stability, the self-development, the self-sufficiency of his essentially rational nature within the social context which provides the occasion for his life and the materials for its fulfillment.

That this picture of "man as man" is at heart the image of Apollonian man is not at first sight evident. For there is no doubt a truth in the view that men taken by and large, and neglecting individual differences, are capable of a kind of rational self-control which no other animal attains. Couple this with the persistent recognition of individual differences which is found throughout Aristotle as an inheritor of the Greek medical tradition, and it seems persuasive that the way of life for man as man would center around the control of the self by reason. Actually hidden premises are involved and hidden preferences. For it would by no means follow that it is best for each individual, or even for mankind, to give over the control of life to that which differentiates men from other animals; it

would not necessarily be to the advantage of animals with a
physical organ which no other animal possessed to favor the
unrestrained growth of that organ or its dominance over all
other organs. Aristotle himself remarks that the object of moral
choice is that which after deliberation is preferred to something else—and the introduction of preference gives the case
away. For it is by no means clear that individuals of different
types will all prefer after deliberation a life of reason in which
they become Apollonians in an Apollonian society. The fact
that all men are in some distinctive sense "rational" does not in
itself determine the way of life they will choose after deliberation, nor the place they will allow to "reason" in this chosen
life. To condemn these alternative choices as "irrational" is
simply to indicate another preference. It is significant that Aristotle banishes the non-Apollonian types of persons with epi-
thets: "could a man be found who takes no pleasure in anything and to whom all things are alike, he would be far from
being human at all"; "the very ugly, or ill-born, or solitary"
are not "capable of happiness"; "as the bad man is easily
changeable, bad must be also the nature that craves change."
Buddhists, Dionysians, Prometheans simply turn out to be "bad
men"; Christian love and Mohammedan zeal would similarly
arise from "excess." They are all deviations from "essential
human nature," that is, from the Apollonian personality—from
Aristotle.

The preference for Apollonian man is strikingly brought out
in Aristotle's attempt to find a criterion for the morality of an
act in the doctrine of the mean. That morality is sought in the
avoidance of excess and in the attainment of a mean state between extremes is itself witness of the Apollonian note of
moderation and harmony. But more lies beneath the surface.
It is recognized that the search for the right act is relative to

particular situations, and that it is to be guided by the use of reason operating within such a situation. So far the doctrine is compatible, say, with the Promethean interpretation of morality which Dewey gives. But Aristotle does not keep to the concrete particular situation for the control of the hypothesis as to what is right in that situation; we instead meet the doctrine that only the good man (who is even said "to be the measure of everything") can determine what is right in the situation; and of course this good man turns out to be the individual who himself approves of moderation, stability, participation in society, rational self-control. An apparent exception serves to underline the point: in one place Aristotle speaks with approval of the man who "will prefer a brief and a great joy to a tame and enduring one." But the context makes clear that the man referred to is one who sacrifices himself for his country or friends: the approval is the Apollonian approval of the warrior defending the existing cultural patterns, and it opens no door of justification for the "excesses" of other types of personality.

The whole of the Aristotelian ethics turns out to rest on the assumption that the Apollonian type of man is the "natural man," and that the institutions and outlook of an Apollonian culture alone are in accordance with the nature of things. Such men and such a culture are made the custodians of the good life. In them Being has shown through Becoming, and Truth through Opinion. Other types of men and other cultures are but preludes or postludes, failures to attain or deviations from the natural. That under the Apollonian cosmology of "essential nature" there is a preference for a type of man, and consequently for certain forms of existence rather than others, is something which the devotee of Apollo can hardly be expected to see—but which others must see. For while the Apollonian type of personality need not apologize for his existence, other types in self-defense must discern the devices by which they are pushed aside as "unnatural." To them at least it will be liberating to recognize Aristotle as the expression and apologist for Apollonian man; nothing less (and this is much)—but nothing more.

The Apollonian temperament has received expression in various cultures. Its features are clear in the cult of Vishnu and in Confucianism; they appear confusedly in Aquinas' Aristotelianized version of Christianity; they are discernible in the pause of Western culture at the period of the Enlightenment. The type of person involved should now be clear. The Apollonian is an active type of person in whom the promethean component is dominant but held in check by a rather strong buddhistic component. The dionysian tendencies of the biologic level are lowest in strength, and attain a relatively easy social redirection. The result is an individual who, in a stable society, is not given to severe conflicts. He lives outwardly in his feelings and actions and thoughts. He is inclined to friendship rather than to strong love, to compromise rather than radical reform, to self-control in the world rather than withdrawal from it. He is particularly able in administration, and except in periods of very rapid social change the reins of society tend to pass into his hands and the forms of society to mirror his image. As long as his security is not seriously threatened, his attitude to others is kindly and even tolerant, his inherent possessiveness is tempered by liberality, and his detachment and objectivity give a judicial aristocratic mien to his self-assurance. He is the gentleman, the judge, the statesman. When secure in his social dominance, his life attains the poise, the easy co-ordination, and the self-control embodied in the idea of classical harmony.

The weakness of this personality and a society dominated by it arises from the fact that the inherent self-centeredness of the Apollonian is dependent upon the control of social agencies and goods for its support; to possess himself he must possess society. For all his apparent detachment, his control of himself is dependent upon his control of things and persons. The strength of this attachment to the present forms of actuality shows the immense distance which separates his characteristic "self-sufficiency" from Buddhistic self-sufficiency: he is centered in the present; the Buddhist is centered only in himself. When the world to which the Apollonian is attached tends to dissolve, he begins (as is evidenced in Plato) to show anxiety, to feel with Dante that "the last age of the world is at hand," to become repressive and tyrannical. His latent hostility to all other types of personality now comes out in the open, for they all seem to him agencies of social dissolution—and so of his own personal dissolution. From a nobly conserving force he becomes an inflexible reactionary force. At first he will only try to hold fast to what exists (he will say, "to what is good"): he will grope for an intellectual system by which he can persuade others that his way is *the* way; he will believe that the agencies of education (the schools, the arts, literature) have failed to inculcate the truths which are in his possession; past human achievements are presented in a way which tends to stifle the new gropings of the now insurgent alien types of personality; he may begin to whimper that all is lost because the human mass was too stupid to follow his insights—forgetting in an all too human way the inherent sterility of his own attitude when life demands basic shifts in vision and tactics. Sooner or later he will be tempted to turn to drastic measures that at least give an outward sense of stability to the social structure. If he does not himself turn muscle-man, he tends to call in the muscle-men to his aid. And that too—though he notices it not —is the death sentence of the Apollonian ideal.

If Aristotle presents the Apollonian ideal in its high form, with only a nod in the direction of Buddhism, Plato shows the Mohammedan direction of its disintegration: Athens has summoned Sparta; Apollo is in distress.

A consideration of Christianity is beset with many difficulties: the brief historic career of its founder makes it difficult to disentangle the germinal doctrines and motivations. At the start it was embedded in, and, indeed, carried on, the religion of Judaism; its subsequent development was deeply influenced by the religious forces operative in the Hellenistic, Islamic, Roman, and northern European environments to which it was transplanted. There are Buddhistic, Dionysian, Promethean, Apollonian and Mohammedan facets of the historical Christianity, and these may easily be confused with what is essential and distinctive. Nevertheless, there is a recognizable Christian path of life, answering to a preferred type of man, which cannot be reduced to the paths already discussed. Christ's personality has been the core around which this version of ideal man has been built, and a peculiar and distinctive form of love rightly has been singled out as the key component in the attitude of Christian man. The Christian path of life is the path of such love; a unique attitude of love is the keystone in the entire development, providing a distinctive color and direction and norm which has persisted throughout diverse emphases and deviations.

What is the nature of this love to be borne to God and neigh-
bor "with all thy heart, and with all thy soul, and with all
thy mind, and with all thy strength?" The term 'love' does not
in itself give the key, for there are as many forms of love as
there are types of personality: for the Dionysian, love takes
the form of an elemental and impersonal passion in which consciousness of the self and consciousness of the other are obliter-
ated in a mystical annihilation; for the Promethean, love is a
form of the constant renewal of the creative self, subordinated
to the eternal remaking in which the beloved becomes material
to be utilized, molded, and relinquished; for the Apollonian,
love, because of its tendency to excessiveness, is intrinsically
inferior to friendship. Christian love, on the contrary, is turned
outward, centered on the beloved; the beloved is raised to the
focus of consciousness, and is magnified, worshiped, adored;
the lover, in contrast, keeps an awed distance, depreciates himself, dedicates himself to the service of the loved one. There
is something of the excessiveness, the transforming power of
the "grand passion" in Christian love with its note of suffering, its self-purification, its self-dedication, its self-transforma-
tion, its ecstatic centering of the self in the other. Those to
whom love has appeared in this form—even if for only a moment—will understand the deep and perennial appeal of Christ,
the burning pages of Augustine's *Confessions*, the tenderness
of St. Francis, the ever-recurring monastic reforms within
historical Christianity, the deeply ingrained core of Christian
mysticism, the exclamation of Aquinas that "this love of God
. . . overflows, and . . . is like a furnace." Others will miss
the dionysian undertones of Christian love, confusing it with
asceticism (as did Nietzsche), or diluting it into a moralistic
doctrine (as did Kant).

The short length of Christ's period of teaching and the early transference of Christianity to the Hellenistic world have made it very difficult to recover the original content of Christ's orientation. But in terms of contemporary scholarship it seems likely that it consisted essentially in the belief that the salvation of the individual, and consequently of mankind, was to be found in a *change of heart*, prefigured in the Psalms: the individual was to be dominated by a unique form of love, extended to God and embracing man. The ascetic element was not advocated for its own sake but to permit such love to be the guiding feature of one's life: the relinquishment of force, the recognition of one's sinfulness, the need for a repentant attitude, the giving up of possessions, the withdrawal from the ordinary round of social relations and ritual were all phases of the purification of the self in order that it might be dominated by such love. The basic point was that this change of heart was felt to be all-sufficient for human redemption; given this attitude of love, God would effect the appearance of the kingdom of heaven in the individual and among men, here on the earth itself. There was no supplementary appeal to such cultural agencies as science or art or technology; the orientation of the person around love was alone essential. There was in this attitude no general depreciation of life, no harsh asceticism, no eye blind to beauty and loveliness; Christ's heart was an overflowing heart and restraint was but the shield of its love.

The Christian path of love is the consequence of allowing such love the dominant role in the self, and of believing in its self-sufficiency. The restraining of the biological self (Paul's crucifixion of "the physical nature with its propensities and cravings") is an agency in permitting such dominance, and in prohibiting love from passing on to a Dionysian or Promethean or Apollonian form; it is the means by which the Christian attempted to give to his life as a whole the character of a grand

and prevailing passion, and to prevent the wonder, the release from self, the sublimity of the initial stages of this passion from dissolution through the release of tension and the return of the self to its everyday workaday world. Through such restraint of the biological self the attitude of love was freed to embrace many men and to extend to the wider cosmos. And so freed and extended the struggle for power, the search for earthly possessions, the arrogance of pride, the ostentation of self-exhibitionism, the concern about tomorrow's food and raiment lost their glamour. Filled with superfluity of such love, trusting in its power alone, holding every phase of the self under its control, endeavoring to extend this attitude to all human relationships, singing to God with all their hearts: this became the Christian's way, his road, his life.

The Christian personality (the type symbolized in Christ) would seem to be a person weakest in the promethean component, with a strong dionysian component controlled by even stronger buddhistic traits; he is therefore the mirror image of the Dionysian temperament in which the relative strength of the dionysian and buddhistic components is reversed. The element of detachment in the Dionysian is periodically overcome by the heightened tension and explosive release of the more elemental phases of the biological self; in the Christian this element of detachment is too strong to permit such release; the dionysian impulses are restricted to an extreme utilization of the more sublimated forms of the socially approved attitude of love, and are forced to a level of symbolic expression in the Mass and in the mystical experiences of a union with God. The preference for such sublimated forms of love requires the follower of Christ to withdraw from the social community in so far as its actions are based on other interests and other forms of love, and to imagine an ideal society—here on earth or in the hereafter—in which Christian love will be the dominant attitude of all its members. In this heaven the Christian heart of over-flowing love will meet its worthy object, symbolized by God—the perfect lover, the staff for the present interim, the object of adoration, the rewarder of the devotion directed to him, the conferrer of final blessedness. The Christian, unlike the more promethean and less dionysian Buddhist, does not believe that his goal can be obtained by the manipulation of himself guided by scientific reasoning: he is dependent upon the Beloved for redeeming grace and for confidence in the all-sufficient power of the attitude of love. The Christian God is the analogue of the ideal Christian man; heaven is the environment in which the Christian would obtain the satisfaction of his essential nature; the Christian way is the path to this salvation. In the worldly interim the follower of Christ will prepare himself in fellow-ship with like-minded persons, and through the Bible and the Church in which the path of salvation is presented and institutionalized. In the sacrament of the Mass he symbolizes—and in typical dionysian symbols—his ultimate union with the Beloved. The usually austere Aquinas reveals the dionysian stratum of the Christian heart when he describes this Mass:

> The many marvels of this Feast amaze the mind: it is luscious beyond all dainties, delicious beyond the rarest delicacies, more fragrant than any odor, more pleasing than any form of grace, more desirable than every other food. . . . Therein there is put before us for meat, not, as of old time, the flesh of bulls and of goats, but Christ Himself, our very God. . . . The slave —O, wonder! eats the Flesh of his Incarnate God!

And in this Mass the votary gains the foretaste of that heaven where "the saints possess most fully everything that a man here could seek whether by sinning or by not sinning." It was the vision of that ecstatic consummation which drew from Aquinas, when asked to continue work on his *Summa Theologica*, the words: "I cannot do more; all that I have written seems to me only straw."

The unique service of the Christian way of life is to give religious significance to that phase of the development of personality in which the self finds an object for devotion in the satisfaction of the interests of others. Such devotion, such love, is encouraged to some extent by every society as a means by which the impulses of the individual are regulated through the individual's own considerate concern for the interests of others. In this Christian complication of the social self, morality takes on a new inwardness: the individual does not merely follow certain courses of action approved by the society, but he deliberately and with devotion to others subordinates himself, controls himself, in order to advance the careers of others. The Christian temperament is uniquely capable of raising to a religious intensity the sentiments of kindliness, sympathy, humility with which man as a social being has attempted to subordinate and transform his biological heritage. At the same time this attitude is in inception no narrowly moralistic one. In chaining his biological impulses, the Christian's eye is freed for the outward glance, and detachment widens and amplifies the dionysian sources of his attachment. Christian love is an overflowing love: if it is consistent and unchecked it must follow with loving eye all the intricacies and differences which men and women reveal (hence its tendency to "judge not" and to transcend the boundaries of every actual social group), and must bring the wider universe within its horizon (the stress on "the love of God," the eye open to the beauties and terrors of nature, the note of cosmic adoration and praise). There is room for leisure in this attitude, for contemplation, for rapt attention to the autonomous careers of other things and other persons.

And yet there are grave difficulties in maintaining the Christian attitude. Lacking the promethean utilization of science and technology, attempting to make the attitude of love all-sufficient, the Christian failed to implement his attitude so that it might attain dominance in the world of men. The promethean impulses have sought for other agencies than love alone to satisfy human interests; the buddhistic sources of detachment have refused to confine themselves to what the love-informed eye might discern; other types of men and women have refused, or been unable, to form themselves in the Christian mold. The harassed Christian, in the face of the resistances encountered in other types of persons and in the limitations of his own religious techniques, has been often driven to desperate measures. Scorning at heart the scientific and technological agencies of human control, he has acquiesced unwillingly but persistently in the forms which Promethean and Apollonian man have given to society, and has seen his grand vision watered down to the defense of the existing social order; or he has turned Mohammedan in his distress, forgetting the injunction to judge not, seeking refuge in the brotherhood of the elect, loving in others only what he loved in himself, fanatically imposing his will upon other recalcitrant types of personality in some variety of holy war. When his kingdom on the earth failed to arrive, he turned his glance more eagerly to a future heavenly home, and the love of God, however satisfying in itself, warred with and often sapped his love of man.

The dependence upon the Beloved—inherent in the very core of Christian love—showed its ugly features: the love was not often pure and disinterested; it sought reward; the suppressed biological impulses evolved a new form of spiritual gluttony: the hunger for immortality. The self which had found a way out to others and the wider world was in danger of hugging itself, taking pride in its righteousness, condemning all selves which were not like itself, disapproving of science's attempt to trace the objective course of things, petulantly demanding that the universe center around its own salvation and eternal perpetuation. The self charged with love becomes transformed, when frustrated, into a self loving itself. Christian love at its best commands the respect and admiration which a great passion elicits; its weakness is the analogue of the sentimentality, self-abuse, reproachfulness, petulance, self-love into which the grand passion is likely to fall if consummation is frustrated or too long delayed. The increasing "supernaturalistic" trek of Christianity was one way in which the Christian protected himself against the frustration of his love in the world of man: his God supplied him the perfect lover which the world failed to supply. There is subtlety in this recourse, and consistency; but if the votary of Christ saves in this way his individual love he weakens at the same time the directive force of his attitude for the mundane scene; and heightens his danger, as a person, of acquiescing to the Apollonian or indulging his rancor at men under Mohammedan guidance.

Christian love is love in the grand style; it has brought into human life new values which even now have not expended their great power and beauty. But interest in the interests of others is only one interest in the human self, and the Christian man is only one type of man. Love, Christian love—so to date the record runs—is not enough, save for those few God-intoxicated ones whose full hearts alike resisted acquiescence and rancor.

The Christian sought, as did other seekers of salvation, to ground his path in the nature of the cosmos; men have been most trustful of their own voices when they seem to echo back from sources outside themselves. But it is significant that the Christian mythology and theology and philosophy were elaborated in cultures other than that in which Christ lived—cultures with their own unique character and problems. Paul's world is the Hellenistic world dominated by dionysian cults in which a Saviour suffers death and resurrection that men may be redeemed—and Christ is transformed into this Saviour; Augustine is the heir of the Roman world passing into the hands of the barbarians, and the Church is impressed with the form of Roman "Mohammedan" organization; in the time of Aquinas the Church had succeeded in obtaining a high place in a temporarily stable social order, and Aquinas grafted the Christian outlook upon the Apollonian-tending Church and Aristotelian naturalism; by Luther's period the characteristically promethean forces of northern European men were dominant in the cultural nexus, and in Protestantism the Christian tradition accommodates itself, slowly and hesitantly, to the Promethean outlook; by the time of Kant—the philosophic shadow of Luther —the scientific mentality had won the day, and the Christian love of the great Commandments had been watered down to the moralistic tone of the categorical imperative.

In this process the votary of Christ had, it is true, developed a picture of the world which justified to him the exclusive rightness of his path of life. He saw the cosmic drama as a theater in which the main plot was the salvation of man's immortal soul; he had transformed God into the image of Christian man; by the distinction of faith and knowledge, the Heavenly City and the Earthly City, he had made room for his human activities and his human rational processes; through his Bible and Church he had assured himself that in his hands alone were the keys to salvation. And yet for all the beauty and ingenuity of his results, the Christian did not play the directive role in Western culture; he accommodated himself for the most part to what others were doing, or distorted his own vision in frantic Mohammedan attempts to compel love by the use of force. The detachment which he helped to promulgate became in the hands of the scientists—descendants in part of the monks—the very agency by which a new world picture was pieced together that jarred with his own. The low promethean component in the Christian temperament, and its attempt to transform the world by holding fast to the attitude of love alone, made the Christian an impotent and often pathetic figure in a culture predominantly Promethean. Christianity in northern Europe becàme but a façade to the social structure which the Promethean spirit of the north was building throughout the centuries. And European man went on his way of earthly struggle, conquest, and invention without the formulation in religious terms of his own essentially Promethean attitude.

And yet the pervasive influence of the Christ ideal in Europe cannot be ignored. Christian man and Promethean man confront each other with hostility to be sure—but with the attraction of alien and complementary types. Their common ground can be the acceptance of a moral life nourished by the love of other individuals; the Christian has deepened this conception of love and the Promethean has put at its services his technological resources. The Christian has held before Promethean man the significance of detachment, the promise of eternal activity, and something of the dionysian sense of communion with the wider cosmos; the Promethean has offered to the Christian an anchorage in the human scene and a utilization of human resources which relieve his frequent sense of impotence and isolation. It it is no accident that philosophers and literary men without number (Descartes, Leibniz, Kant, Blake, Goethe, as instances) have tried to unite in some way the images of Prometheus and Christ—neither of which alone has answered fully to the demands of Western men. The joint existence in Western culture of the Promethean and Christian traditions has produced the "magnificent tension" of this culture which Nietzsche noted, and has perhaps laid the ground for a novel and characteristic religious synthesis.

At the threshold of the Koran we meet a separation of men into two groups: believers and unbelievers, "the fellows of the Garden" and "the fellows of the Fire." And this separation is the key to the Mohammedan personality and a Mohammedan culture. The believers constitute a community of the elect, chosen by God and led by his apostle; their task is to follow God and his apostle to victory over the evil forces manifested in the God-rejected unbelievers; as the fruit of this victory they shall inherit the good things of the earth and the future world; their lives are directed through the complete dedication of themselves to the extension of the power of the community. The believers are "submissive" to Allah and Mohammed; but such submission has no trait of negative or passive resignation: it is the abandonment which comes from relinquishing the self-

centered "I" to a communal "we." There is a release from buddhistic restraint in this submission and an outlet for strong action and strong feeling. The discipline which it involves is a
warrior's discipline; it is not the discipline of the ascetic as
such, but the focusing of all one's powers so that the community, and oneself as a member of the community, shall enjoy
now and hereafter the satisfaction of its desires. To members of
the community, kindness, considerateness, moderation; to the
unbelievers who refuse to accept the Word, unremitting warfare,
hostility, death. The community of the elect in fact defines with
its authority the sphere of individual obligation: the community
determines with respect to its cause what the individual is to
do, what he is to believe, what he is to regard as good and evil.
Drinking, amusements, niggardliness, individualistic art, numerous possessions, suicide, the accentuation of the family—these
weaken the cohesion of the community, and are condemned in
the Koran; prayer, almsgiving, pilgrimages, kindliness to the
fellow elect—these increase the sense of intimate relation with
the community, and are approved.

These disapprovals and approvals are expressed through the
leader, the apostle, and are felt to have a cosmic source: Allah
is the patron and guardian of the believers, and shall lead them
to victory over the unbelievers; as the one God, he is without
opposition, and the kindness which he deals to the elect is
matched by the terror with which he metes out destruction and
damnation to the unbelievers. Those who war in his name shall
enjoy now the goods of the earth and in the hereafter the peace,
the shade, the upraised beds, the wine and fruit which cause
no indigestion, the perpetual virgins of the Gardens; the God-
rejected unbelievers who resist Allah's dominion shall suffer
eternally the hot blasts, the pitchy smoke, the boiling water, the
ever-renewed fires of hell. Allah's victory is certain; he has sent

his grace "to tie up your hearts and to make firm your foot-
steps"; tied to "the rope of God" and the rope of the community of believers, the individual loses his self-centered life to
find new life in the company of the elect. The elect, and only
the elect, shall be saved: "Whosoever craves other than Islam
for a religion, it shall surely not be accepted from him, and he
shall in the next world be of those who lose"; but "whoso fights
in God's way . . . be he killed or be he victorious, we will give
him a mighty hire."

The relation of the apostle to the community is a double one.
As a member of the community, embodying in concrete form its
approvals and disapprovals, he links his life with its tasks, its
victories, its defeats. Mohammed loved perfumes, food, women;
yet he avoided luxury in clothes and dwellings, he directed his
own armies, he put his hand to the pick to turn the ground for
trenches, he prohibited the ceremonies in his favor from taking
the form of worship. As the leader of the group he is one with
the group; and yet, as the apostle of God, he has a place apart.
Half man, half god, he holds himself aloof. Easy familiarity
with him is frowned upon; his name is not to be used; special
privileges—as in his relation to women—accrue to him; a per-
centage of all the spoils of war go to him. As the elect of the
elect, the destiny of the community is in his hands. He is at once
prophet, warrior, ruler, and judge. He can set aside former
customs: Mohammed sanctioned attacks by his followers on
unarmed caravans during religious periods when arms were not
to be carried; he proclaimed that captivity annuls marriage; to
the Apollonian query as to whether men should not "follow
their fathers," the Koran replies: "What! though their fathers
knew nothing and were not guided!" The new decreed ways are,
however, in their turn made absolute. The rise of new prophets
with divergent doctrines is discounted in advance with an in-

genious artifice: Allah is supposed to have assembled all past, present, and future prophets, and to have secured their approval of the doctrines announced in the Koran: "He who turns back after that, these are sinners." The future is thereby bound: there is nothing of the Promethean belief in a future to be eternally made anew; the goal is in the future, to be sure, but the form of this future is determined in advance; there is one God, one Truth, one Way. And the prophet, as the emissary of God, the holder of the Truth, and the pointer of the Way speaks with the voice of authority. The figure of Allah which informs the Koran is in actuality the projection of the personality of Mohammed; the submission to Allah is in effect submission to Mohammed.

It is not difficult to discern the major outlines of the Mohammedan type of personality: the dionysian components are strongest; these are directed and partially controlled by the strongly developed promethean component; the buddhistic factors are the weakest of all. The Mohammedan lives outwardly and lacks a center of orientation within himself. He needs a "rope" to tie to—a community with an authoritative leader to be followed—and given such a rope he leads a life of high physical and emotional intensity. He delights in sensuous enjoyment, strong passion, primitive emotions, but because of his high promethean and low buddhistic inclinations these will take an objective social form. His emotional life will follow and color his active strivings; his joy is a warrior's joy which needs the support of fellow warriors combating a common enemy. He delights in feeling himself the agency of elemental forces; he is never far from a magical outlook in which dreams, "jinns," superstition, omens, play a great role; the "life of reason" has no claims upon him. Solitude is foreign to his nature, as are Buddhistic minimization of the self, or Dionysian festivals outside of the main social group, or Christian injunctions to love the enemy. Apollonian detachment and moderation are alien to him, and the Promethean discontent with every present. If his "holy war" requires a warrior's discipline, this merely involves the projection to a distant future of his present self: the Garden will be such as to satisfy his present inclinations, and he will indulge his existing, though temporarily disciplined, cravings when he enters its friendly gate.

The power of the Mohammedan personality, given fellow companions, a leader, and an enemy, is manifestly great. Lacking internal conflicts and inhibitions, employing the elemental force of primitive passions and actions, feeling that he is the vehicle of a cosmic destiny which defines all that opposes his community as evil, willing to utilize any means to reach his goal, enjoying the free expenditure of his available energy, confident of the outcome of his exertions, the Mohammedan can only appear as a terror, a scourge, a "beast" to other types of personality. Indeed, in periods of Mohammedan dominance, these other types are liable to cut a pathetic figure. In one way or another, like the Buddhists in the face of the Mohammedan invasion of India, they fall before his sword. Either they are deficient in the promethean forces which could oppose resistance (as in the case of the Buddhists, Christians, and Dionysians) or they combine with these forces an element of detachment which prevents the quick and effective utilization of such forces (as in the case of the Apollonians and Maitreyans). Nor is it difficult to see why periodically the Mohammedans come to power. The institutions of a society constantly tend to harden, to fossilize, to become formal, to face disruptive dangers from within and without; more and more individuals fail to find in the society a life adequate to their natures; the Mohammedan under such circumstances gains his power and gives to the society the sense of goal, integration, vitality by releasing the oldest and most persistent features of the human self and by enlisting moral sentiments and group loyalty in the service of a holy war; all that makes for detachment, isolation, doubt is removed, and life, though still socially oriented, is simplified and led by the imperious sway of emotionalized action.

Yet, the Mohammedan has never conquered the earth, and the empires he has erected have dissolved. There are weaknesses in his personality, and forces which undermine his power. Lacking self-centeredness, the Mohammedan is dependent upon finding a leader who can hand down a rope, organize a community, and isolate the enemy. The strength of the Mohammedan lies in the leader, the community, and the enemy; as an individual he has not the inventive skill, the foresight, the inner resourcefulness, the organizational skill of some of his opponents. He is led by a leader, and the leader who gives the original impetus is more visionary, electric, solitary than the typical Mohammedans he brings into power. The leaders who take up his task may be even more efficient, more ruthless, than he, and they may long draw upon the capital (the "merit") which he accumulated. But they are less able to understand and to seduce opposing types of personality, or to utilize long their services. They even attempt to exterminate their rivals; but they have not been able—in the past at least—to do the job thoroughly enough to perpetuate their own survival. The original impulse wavers, the needed enemy has perhaps been vanquished, the far-flung empire becomes a shell, the non-Mohammedans silently give new content to the formal structure. Thinking continues to go on, the Promethean insensibly modifies the technical resources of the community, love continually spills over the walls which separate the elect from the damned, the suppressed buddhistic phase of the human self seeks for some outlet. At the same time, with deterioration in leadership, the Mohammedans lose the mystic bond of unity which gives them strength, and since they cannot stand alone upon their own feet, with all their show of external pomp and power they become easily disorganized when they lack a leader able to electrify them.

In the past the dissolution of Mohammedan empires has been aided by the growth in other regions of the earth of peoples with greater technological resources than those developed by the empire; and a genuinely Promethean society offers the major opposition to the unlimited spread of Mohammedan conquest. Were an earth-wide Mohammedan empire to be achieved, commanding all technological agencies and breeding individuals to its needs, the prediction of the Koran would have been achieved: "Verily, we will inherit the earth and all who are upon it."

In the nature of the case, the Mohammedan type of personality, weak in the forces making for detachment, is not disposed toward a philosophic elaboration and justification of his attitude. There is no equally prominent philosopher who stands in a relation to this way of life as does Aristotle to the Apollonian, Gautama Buddha to the Buddhist, Augustine to the Christian, Nietzsche to the Dionysian, Dewey to the Promethean. Machiavelli has, it is true, given a handbook to the Mohammedan leader, and the pages of Hobbes have offered him much to his purpose, but in neither case does he find there the cosmic justification for the mission which so completely and fanatically fills his being. He is forced therefore to content himself with opposition to philosophies alien to himself, and with turning to his own account philosophies which provide a stirrup in which he can insert his own foot. In the contemporary world he has found in Marx and in Nietzsche material which he could mold and assimilate to his own attitude.

Marx himself was an essentially Promethean figure, extending to the control of human society the same restless, realistic, constructional attitude by which Promethean man has, in science and technology, bent the processes of physical nature to his will. He was a technologist operating on man as his material, aware of the objectivity which the scientific attitude requires, attentive to the natural context in which men live and the agencies by which men seek to fulfill their needs, suspicious of metaphysical systems which assert their superiority to scientific knowledge, driven by the belief that men through understanding and effort can improve their lot. Marx's thought was, in the main, part of the naturalistic transformation of philosophy with which Western man has accompanied the slowly gained recognition of his predominantly Promethean nature.

And yet the stirrups for Mohammedan feet are there. The conception of the dialectic process, taken over from Hegel and regarded as the substitute for metaphysics, lent itself to the formulation of another, and rival, metaphysics. The dialectical process by which matter spews out new forms of existence takes the place of the will of Allah, dealing good and evil alike; Marx is made into the apostle; the proletariat becomes the brotherhood of the elect, chosen by dialectical matter as the vehicle of its contemporary expression; submission to the party —the rope of the new Islam—replaces submission to Allah and Mohammed; the *bourgeoisie* plays the role of the enemy unbelievers; the "holy war" is the war of the elect against the unbelievers for the control of the earth; all forms of force are sanctioned which advance the cause; art, science, morality, truth, are defined within the limits of the proletariat class; the elect are promised the good things of the earth; the "classless society" is the Garden—and Siberia the proper place of abode for such "fellows of the Fire" as are permitted to survive. The whole movement takes on the character of a religious crusade; the pattern of salvation is Mohammedan in all its essential features. The persons to whom the appeal is directed and for whom it is most persuasive are the workers and the youths, accustomed to physical activity, anxious for the satisfactions and comforts of elemental needs frustrated by enslavement to the machine or by lack of employment, unattracted by buddhistic detachment. The Christian also feels this appeal, at least in the initial stages of the movement, for it promises him an object for his love, to which he can give himself; and it enlists the restless forces of those Prometheans whom the Apollonian facet of society tends to restrict if not to frustrate. But the actual leadership of the movement passes, or tends to pass, into the hands of the men of steel—the Stalins replace the Marx's, and the old words are spoken with new accents by new tongues.

A somewhat similar situation occurs in the Fascist-Nazi utilization of Nietzsche: the elect and the enemy differ, but the pattern is otherwise the same. There was in Nietzsche himself a joy in solitude, intellectual analysis, aesthetic detachment. The promethean note, the sense for technology, was, we have argued, submerged in the call to Dionysus with which Nietzsche hoped to break through his anchorite walls, and yet it was there, supplemented and confused by approving words for the Platos, the Napoleons, the Cesare Borgias, and the new Spartan tyrants whom the age of nihilism was to rear. The Mohammedans took these words to heart and saw themselves as the leaders of the elect to whom Nietzsche called. Tracks were traced between Berlin and Weimar, Rome and Weimar. The apologists made Nietzsche over, suppressing what was alien to the Mohammedan image, bringing to the forefront what coincided with its figure. The unbelievers were located: near at hand the Jews and the Communists, farther afield the democracies. The Apollonians were captured by promises that the new movement would save them from the perils of Communism and Communistic forces in the democracies; the dionysian and promethean tendencies of the young were tied with a new rope, co-ordinated and released. Force was used to band every energy and every personality to the leader's will. Hesitancy, division of the rich and poor, doubt were burned in the forge of resolution, determination, unity. Internationalism, scientific detachment, individualistic art, alternative religions were subjugated by the community of the elect. Spengler helped betray the Promethean to the Mohammedan: himself seeking the detachment of the Apollonian generalized to behold all cultures, the effect of his doctrine upon others was to convince them that the dying energies of Promethean man would take their final form in Caesarean hands. Hitler crystallized the whole movement in a deed; the parallel to Mohammed is complete almost to the smallest detail; *Mein Kampf* is a modern Koran. Hitler rejects the Christian view of the ultimate significance of the individual human soul; the stress is on "magic insight" rather than the "random path of intelligence," on fighting rather than passivity, and on "ecstatic and fanatic" masses freed from the burden of objectivity.

Roped to new books and new apostles, fresh Mohammedan

bands have set out to conquer the earth. The words and the warriors are different; the patterns and the cycles are as of old.

The Apollonian, Christian, and Mohammedan attitudes have a common feature: they seek salvation through society; in this respect they are in contrast to the more individualistic techniques for salvation of the Buddhist, the Dionysian, and the Promethean. These latter attitudes, in spite of their emphasis on the self as center, hug the self less tightly than do the votaries of Apollo, Christ and Mohammed; while their followers are more solitary, less inherently social, the techniques they employ involve the relinquishment of self: the Buddhist, through contemplation of his nature, gives the components of his self back to the universe, the Promethean loses himself in his restless activity of making, the Dionysian seeks an orgiastic release from the burden of selfhood. In all these cases other persons may be used, but used as means for the return to self that the self may be laid down. Loneliness, cosmic vision, an open universe, essential homelessness, renunciation of self: these are the common themes.

The Apollonians, the Christians, the Mohammedans are, on the contrary, socially centered, and their vision is of a society in which their socially attained and socially dependent selves may be affirmed and zealously preserved. The Christian is lost without his Heavenly Father and Heavenly City; the Mohammedan is dependent upon his Leader for entrance into the Garden; the Apollonian is frantic as the social structure in which he finds his status dissolves. These-persons all clutch the self and hunger for some form of immortality; they bind the future to a determinate form; their outlook is at heart conservative, epochal, closed, finite, time-centered. They bear witness to the need of incorporating into a plan of salvation the social matrix in which the human self has arisen and in which it operates. They are the guardians of the social strata of the self, and their insights cannot be negated without repudiating the social phases and needs of developed human nature.

The Mohammedan pattern of salvation makes its strongest appeal to a society in great distress. For it offers a means of tying together the resources of a society against the internal and external forces which threaten it. It provides the sense of conviction needed to release resolute action. It turns the loyalties and co-operativeness which morality has encouraged to the service of the goals of an integrated society. It furnishes a highly dynamic society which is willing to make drastic changes in itself in order to gear itself to its problems. It thus seems progressive, mighty, and irresistible. But, as we have seen, its power is obtained through a radical simplification of the self and society; it leaves unsatisfied much of the self it promises to employ and to save. And for all its sense of bigness with the future, the future society it envisages is a static one, an ever-enduring society whose form and content are fixed in advance.

The Apollonian society is more genial, more open, more tolerant; it is the society of Aristotle's *Politics* in contrast to the more Mohammedan society of Plato's *Republic* or Hitler's *Mein Kampf*. It has room for cultural diversity, individual differences, the free play of intelligence. Its virtue is the preservation and the appreciation of what has been attained; its vice is its inability to envisage new insights and to make drastic changes where these are necessary; its danger is to turn Mohammedan as its security is threatened. The strength of its attachment to the past and present saps its allegiance to the future.

The Christian society is, of the three forms in question, the society most open to the future. It delineates an attitude to control the future and it dreams of a society in which this attitude will in time become the dominant attitude of all men, but the details of this society are fortunately indefinite. It has made itself the guardian of the social impulses of the self without too narrowly determining the outward form which these impulses must assume. The great strategic strength of the Christian tradition lies in the variability of its manifestations. We have seen how it adapted itself to Dionysian, Apollonian, Mohammedan, Promethean epochs; it is fitted to perform a similar role in the transition to a Maitreyan epoch. Its essential emphasis upon the dignity of the human self commits it, if it is consistent, to the extension of its attitude of love to all types of persons and to a society in which all such types can function. If one is to love men, and if men differ, one must love the differences in men. Institutionalized Christianity must now in its own expansive advance again transform the Christ type of personality; this is its fate and its imperious mission.

In its historical movement, Christianity has shown two faces: if it has many times made peace with the Apollonian and Mohammedan, it has also perennially sought to keep alive the freer future consistent with the amplitude of its generating love. This has led the Christian, however slowly and hesitantly, to borrow from the Promethean techniques to implement and make socially effective his own dominant attitude. This tendency is of decisive cultural importance. For the Christian and the Promethean types complement each other in respect to the personality traits each emphasizes. In so far as promethean impulses are allowed to operate, the personality obtains release from the inhibitive conflict imposed by the juxtaposition of dionysian and buddhistic traits in the Christ type of personality. The frustrations, the sentimentality, the rigidity, the impotence engendered in this stalemate drop away, and Christian love is freed to operate through the whole personality, and to use all the instrumentalities which mind and body and emotion make available. In their mutual contact, Christian and Promethean budge each other in the direction of Maitreyan man. If Christianity can remain faithful to the range of its initial vision, retain the adaptability evidenced in its historical career, and avoid acquiescence to Apollonian or Mohammedan wisdom, it can, at least in the West of this round earth, help prepare the birth of the Maitreyan epoch.

VII. The Maitreyan Path of Generalized Detached-Attachment

"He who seeth inaction in action, and action in inaction, he is wise among men, he is harmonious, even while performing all action."

The Bhagavad-Gita

"Both in and out of the game, and watching and wondering at it."

Whitman: *Leaves of Grass*

VII

The Maitreyan Path of Generalized
Detached-Attachment

THE major historical forms of religion are incomplete: there has not been formulated a way of life expressive of the type of personality in which the dionysian, promethean, and buddhistic components of temperament are all fairly strong and of approximately equal strength. We have called this the Maitreyan personality; the corresponding religious attitude will be designated as Maitreyism, for reasons to be discussed as the argument proceeds. Since this personality has not yet found its embodiment in a religious prophet nor its embellishment and delineation in literature and philosophy, it is difficult at this time to focus sharply the picture of Maitreyan man. But the possibility of such a personality is evident, and certain of his features are even now discernible. We must do something to fix them before our attention, and investigate the consequences of taking Maitreyan man as an ideal human type around which to build a philosophy, a religion, and a society.

The essential characteristic of the Maitreyan lies in his need to accept and to integrate all of the features of the human self which in various ways are given unequal supremacy in the other types of personality. He is at once strongly promethean, dionysian, and buddhistic. He will by nature understand and sympathize with the six types of personality and six types of religious attitude which have already been surveyed, but he will be unable to take as his ideal or his religion any of these types

of persons or any of their directive attitudes. They will all seem
to him to have stressed something essential to the development
of the full human self, and yet to have distorted some phase of
this self by giving it exclusive dominance. The friendliness of
his attitude to other personalities will be tempered by a critical
rejection of each of them when proposed as models for human
life. He will wish to incorporate the significance which men
and women have found in the Buddha, Dionysus, Prometheus,
Apollo, Christ, and Mohammed, but he will be unable to take
any of these man-gods as his supreme deity. A Maitreyan of the
present epoch will wish to incorporate in his synthesis the complex levels of the self which man as man has acquired in the
process of social evolution and which have received objective
expression in the arts, in science, and in moral and material
technologies. Yet he will wish to utilize the deep and persistent
biological heritage of man; and he will be attentive to individual differences and loyal to the differences which distinguish
him from other individuals. He will have to delineate an attitude
characteristic of his own individuality, and to trace the intellectual and aesthetic and cultural implications of this attitude.
He will have to build his own distinctive religious orientation.

To other types of persons the Maitreyan will seem no distinctive type: they will regard him as trying to be all—and becoming nothing. He will appear as too detached and restrained
to those of more imperative dionysian and promethean impulses,
too active, sensuous, mystic, abandoned to more buddhistic persons. He will seem to have made too much concession to society
to those who float their ship through throwing over the social
cargo; he will seem too individualistic, anarchic, revolutionary
to those who seek salvation on the social raft. The radicals will
link him with the conservatives and the conservatives with the
radicals. The West will find him too oriental and the Orient too

occidental. The scholars will find him an insufficient intellectualist, and the artists and men of action will find him too scientific. He will, at once, though from different points of view, seem too balanced and too chaotic.

His own doubts will beset him from within. Pulled in three directions by his dionysian, promethean, and buddhistic steeds, the Maitreyan will have his torments in keeping the reins in his hands. These divergent activities cannot, in fact, be to the same degree simultaneously operative. In the variations of their expression, the Maitreyan will often seem to himself, as well as to others, to be simply the chameleonlike Proteus—one type of person at one moment and another type at another moment. Indeed, to some extent this is his fate, but even if this were the whole story there would be something distinctive in his attitude: it would exemplify flexibility, and it would provide a perspective by which the chasms which divide various types of personalities could be bridged. Yet the Maitreyan will not admit that he is only Proteus. Even when he, for instance, assumes the mask of Dionysus he cannot completely disown the voices of the other gods, and his resulting attitude is his own, and to him more than a pale approximation to the attitude of more inflexible devotees; his "chaos" will have its own intense form of dynamic (and often tragic) balance; his own attitude is not resolvable into the successive assumption of other attitudes nor into their mathematical summation. And if he inevitably is to encounter opposition, he can understand the source of this opposition; in making himself the guardian of the complexity of the full human self he can at least be sure that at some point and to some degree he will join hands with those who stress some portion of this self, and some historical phase of its evolution; an understanding of the relation of paths of life to types of personality will give him strength to elaborate a way of life congenial to himself.

This will in the nature of the case take time. The advance will require sorties from various points of vantage. Many persons will have to chisel on the image. There will be internal disagreements and external misunderstandings and opposition. Impetus will be given by the fact that for many persons the old ways of life have proved insufficient, and need will nourish their inventiveness; courage will come with the realization that many omens point in the new direction and that human advance is as much dependent on the reformulation of ideals as it is upon the improved realization of such ideals as already exist. Such is the course of every path of life. And the universe is lavish with time.

It is unwise to be dogmatic at this period of history in characterizing the dominant attitude of the Maitreyan. Nevertheless there are grounds for believing that this attitude is suggested, if not exhausted, in the ideal of generalized detached-attachment. For it would seem as though an attachment to all phases of the self would require at the same time an attitude of detachment to any particular phase of the self in order to prevent it from usurping the active expression of other phases. The resulting attitude would involve both detachment and attachment, generalized to embrace each phase of the self, and extended to the whole self, to the universe, and to the attitude of detached-attachment itself.

The apparent contradiction in such an attitude is easily dispelled. It is true that attachment is coextensive with desire, so that it is impossible for the same interest to be at once

concerned for an object and unconcerned about it. But it is not
at all impossible to have different attitudes to the same object.
Thus a person may be loved intensely because of ministering
to some interests, and yet be hated intensely in relation to other
interests—hated, for instance, because the very dependence upon
the person loved puts the lover in some sense at the mercy of
the beloved. Such a situation may lead to an impasse, in that the
love and the hate may prevent either interest from being satisfied, but it need not do so. This would not be the case if one
of the interests is of a higher order than the other, that is,
includes the other interest as an object. The lover may be
deeply attached to the beloved, but he may wish to protect these
very interests from frustration due to the possible death or
change of attitude of the loved one. The beloved now becomes
an object of scrutiny, and the love is lived in the light of the
possibility of its partial or complete frustration; a note of
wariness, of detachment, has entered. A new and complex
attitude has developed which involves both attitudes of attachment and detachment. The attachment is not simply indulged;
it is allowed to function in the light of an understanding of
its nature and the conditions of its fulfillment or frustration.
Similar illustrations might be drawn in connection with the
sense of humor, the attitude of sportsmanship which the game
has developed, and the peculiar combination of objectivity and
intimacy which friendship demands.

It is the fact that desires occur at various levels, the higher
order desires including the lower level ones among their objects, which makes possible the attitude of detached-attachment,
and keeps it from being either a contradiction, or the mere lock-
ing of opposed attitudes to the same object, or the bare alternation in time of attitudes incompatible at a given time. The
attitude of generalized detached-attachment is *an* attitude

though it contains component attitudes; and since it may function at any level in the hierarchy of interests which make up the self, it may become the dominant attitude of the self and the basis of its orientation. Nothing more is needed for it to serve as a religious attitude, nor to explain how it may take up into itself something of the attitudes characteristic of other religions.

The attitude of attachment to an object is of course changed in the process of being incorporated in an attitude of detached-attachment to that object. But the intensity of the attachment—though no longer blind and without reservation—is not necessarily weakened in this incorporation. It of course may be, and then the attitude of detached-attachment has simply passed over into an attitude of detachment to the object in question. But it may even be strengthened: the realization that the loved one will die is in part a preparation against such death, but it may serve to heighten and intensify the love in a way which unquestioning affection or complete confidence as to the continued availability of the loved one could never do. Detachment does not then in general weaken the strings of attachment. Indeed it proves to be no rival to attachment, but an instrument in the service of attachment itself.

The previous discussion of Buddhism and of Christianity is relevant at this point, and the whole story of the way in which scientific detachment has ministered to the techniques by which man has sought control of himself and the world. The detachment involved, for instance, in the aesthetic attitude does not negate values but allows them to stand out for more vivid inspection; the detachment involved in the moral life serves the same function with respect to the interests of other persons. To seek detachment, even detached-attachment, is itself a form of attachment. Even the desire for death (for detachment from life), when it exists, may be an attempt to make oneself impregnable by accepting and affirming what reflection has convinced one is inevitable: to love death would be to attain a desire certain to be realized.

The acceptance of the attitude of generalized detached-attachment simply raises to the level of conscious orientation the wariness which life has developed in the face of a world which limits and terminates life's essential insurgence. At the simplest biological level one finds its prototype in a dual system of opposed functions which on the one hand drives the animal forward to expansive and aggressive behavior, and on the other hand prepares it for opposition, for defense, and for retreat. Both aid the total life economy of the organism. If the first tendency were to become too dominant, life would hurl itself irresponsibly into a world it could not assimilate; if the latter tendency were too strong, life would starve itself by its inability to grasp the sources of its nourishment. When the self has grown its social superstructure, and the processes of reflection thus made possible, it can fuse these polar attitudes of attachment and detachment into a single whole. It has done this to a degree in science, in art, in morality, in humor, in the game, in friendship. When it has raised the attitude of detached-attachment to the focal point of orientation, extending it to all components and to all levels of the self, it has laid the basis for a new religious attitude.

Though the attitude of generalized detached-attachment has not been raised historically to the rank of a religious attitude, and exemplified in the life of a religious prophet, it has received at least a partial expression in many religions and colored the lives of a number of individuals.

Hinduism is a peculiarly instructive case. This oldest of the great institutionalized religions is often criticized by rival religions for its broad tolerance and its wide eclectic tendencies. But from our point of view these traits are but the consequence of the enlightened manner in which it has made provision for the differences in individuals and the corresponding features of the universe to which these differences make them attentive. These differences are reflected in its gods and in the various religious paths it recognizes. The path of devotion is provided for the more dionysian natures, the path of action for the more promethean natures, the path of knowledge (into which it assimilated Buddhism) for the more buddhistic natures. The gods of its trinity were regarded as manifestations of the one supreme uncharacterizable God: Siva the destroyer was Dionysian (his ascetic side is witness to the dionysian-buddhistic tension of the Dionysian); Brahma the creator was Promethean (the subordinate role he came to play is evidence of the restricted outlet that promethean impulses had in the oriental environment); Vishnu the preserver incorporated the socially conservative emphasis characteristic of the Apollonian. All paths led to the same goal; all gods were forms of the same god. Psychologically it is evident that there are deep affiliations between Maitreyism and Hinduism, however diverse the cultures in which they operate and the philosophies which they call to their aid.

The attitude of detached-attachment is frequently encountered in Hinduist scriptures. Typical is this passage of the *Bhagavad-Gita*:

Man winneth not freedom from action by abstaining from

activity, nor by mere renunciation doth he rise to perfection. Nor can anyone, even for an instant, remain really actionless; for helplessly is every one driven to action by the qualities born of nature. Who sitteth, controlling the organs of action, but dwelling in his mind on the objects of the senses, that bewildered man is called a hypocrite. But who, controlling the senses by the mind, O Arjuna, with the organs of action without attachment, performeth yoga by action, he is worthy. Perform thou right action, for action is superior to inaction, and inactive, even the maintenance of thy body would not be possible. . . . Without attachment, constantly perform action which is duty, for, by performing action without attachment, man verily reacheth the Supreme.

A Maitreyan would be uneasy at the subordinate role which Dionysus receives in this passage, but he would recognize in it a partial expression of his own attitude of detached-attachment.

He would also find suggestions of this attitude in Buddhistic (and especially in the later Buddhistic) writings:

> Whose heart and mind no attachment hampers
> Whose head and heart love and gladness fill.

> To take an attitude of neither indifference nor
> Attachment toward all things.

> He whose mind is above affirmation and negation,
> Rides permanently in the Buddha vehicle.

> Both action and inaction may find room in thee;
> Thy body agitated, thy mind tranquil,
> Thy soul as limpid as a mountain lake.

> Familiarity singularly tinged with aloofness.

In Taoist writings the attitude of detached-attachment often takes the mild "cosmic" dionysian form, with the consequent under-playing of the element of action, which is characteristic of the religion:

> For the world is a divine vessel:
> It cannot be shaped;
> Nor can it be insisted upon.
> He who shapes it damages it;
> He who insists upon it loses it.
> Therefore the sage does not shape it, so he does not damage it;
> He does not insist upon it, so he does not lose it.

Western man has been much less reluctant to lay his own shaping hands on the "divine vessel" and much more reluctant to restrain his senses and his body. But even here he has groped toward some way of incorporating the attitude of detachment into his life. Art, science, and morality are witnesses that this incorporation has to some degree taken place.

Stoicism and Christianity are more explicit forms of the experiment. Of Christianity we have already spoken at length. Stoicism shows evidence of an attempt to somehow bring together the attitudes of detachment and attachment. Thus Epictetus states:

> It is hard to combine these two qualities, the carefulness of one who is affected by circumstances, and the intrepidity of one who heeds them not. But it is not impossible; else were happiness also impossible. We should act as we do in sea-faring. "What can I do?"—choose the master, the crew, the day, the opportunity. Then comes a sudden storm. What matters it to me? my part has been fully done. The matter is in the hands of another—the Master of the ship. The ship is foundering. What then have I to do? I do the only thing that remains to me—to be drowned without fear, without a cry, without upbraiding God, but knowing that what has been born must likewise perish.

For I am not Eternity, but a human being—a part of the whole, as an hour is part of the day. I must come like the hour, and like the hour must pass!

But taken as a whole Stoicism was more Buddhistic than Maitreyan, the promethean impulses were directed more to the control of the self than to the control of the world, and the dionysian impulses were allowed to appear only in the sublimated form of ultimate "abandonment" to the wider cosmic processes.

W. E. Hocking, reviewing in his *Thoughts on Life and Death* this "experiment in detachment" and the causes of its failure concludes:

> The true result of this Western experiment, as I read it, is that detachment and attachment somehow belong together. . . . It is the principle of duality that is affirmed by this experiment . . . detachment had here entered into an auspicious cooperation with attachment. And our problem is largely what can be meant by such a normal and genuine detachment as neither Stoicism nor early Christianity truly defined.

Hocking's statement that "it is only the detached self that is capable of effective attachment" is supported by such findings as those of Kurt Goldstein, who gives evidence, in his *Human Nature in the Light of Psychopathology*, that psychopathic behavior is accompanied by an inability to incorporate the attitude of detachment into the adjustment to the particular problems set by the immediate environment.

Leonardo da Vinci was a forerunner of the Maitreyan ideal as operative in life. He was at once the scientist seeking minute fidelity in the reports of his observations and experiments, the engineer-inventor engaged in the control and transformation of the physical environment, and painter with eye alert to the iridescence of the instant. With all his endless perceptual and inventive curiosity, this "disciple of experience" delighted at the abstractness of mathematical thought; and over his long life of continual and restless activity is spread the mantle of a poignant detachment.

The same Walt Whitman that sang of working and building America,

> Shapes ever projecting other shapes,
> Shapes of turbulent manly cities,

and knew "the mystic deliria, the madness amorous, the utter abandonment,"

> Through me forbidden voices,
> Voices of sexes and lusts, voices veiled and I remove the veil.
> Voices indecent by me clarified and transfigur'd,

could write in his *Song of Myself*:

> But they are not the Me myself.
> Apart from the pulling and hauling stands what I am,
> Stands amused, complacent, compassionate, idle, unitary,
> Looks down, is erect, or bends an arm on an impalpable certain rest,
> Looking with side-curved head curious what will come next,
> Both in and out of the game and watching and wondering at it.

Such words from the East and the West serve at least to show that the Maitreyan attitude finds an echo in the long history of man's attempt to weave together the cool amplitude of detached vision with the warmth and insistency of his momentary urgencies and activities.

It is a central characteristic of Maitreyism to assume the full burden of the self: to look with grateful eyes upon the dionysian, promethean, and buddhistic impulses of human nature, and to respect man's biological heritage, his social self, and his life of reason. But in generalizing its attachment we have seen that it is forced also to generalize its detachment: no one component of human nature, no one level of the self, is to be allowed to tyrannize over the others. Nor, in being attached to the self as a whole, does the Maitreyan lose his sense of detachment for the whole self. While grateful to the forces which sustain his activity, and energetic in his attempt to ride these forces, he has no illusions as to his place in the wider scheme of the universe; no insistence that he be exempt from the doom which is the fate of all component things, no festering resentment toward forces which prove, after struggle, stronger than he: he sweeps them and himself and all mankind into a vast dionysian festival. Yet he is not falsely humble: he goes his own way without apology; he knows that action, even in the service of love, requires decisions, commitments, preferences, suffering, and struggle; he has renounced his self cosmically only to find it humanly. If in his attachment to all he has found a stable object of affection, in his detachment from all (and from even his detachment) he has discounted and surmounted his ultimate defeat. He has assumed the full burden of the self and laid it down; this is his bid for impregnability; this state of generalized detached-attachment is his salvation.

A religion of this orientation has generalized the attitudes of attachment and detachment, and caught them up into a synthetic and inclusive attitude applicable to all phases of the universe and of the self. If it finds features of merit in all preceding religions, it is not itself a form of any particular historical religion. Why then has a predicted future Buddha been chosen as its patron man-god?

There is a genuine sense in which this religion continues the religious quest where early Buddhism left off. It is true that it does not accept as a general principle the negation of all desires. But even if this principle could without qualification be ascribed to Buddhism—and we have seen that this would have to be done cautiously in the light of Buddhist history with its clear indications of an attitude of detached-attachment—it is by no means the whole of Buddhism. Early Buddhism, as we have seen, sought for a salvation attainable by the individual in his lifetime through self-control guided by a clear understanding of himself and his position in nature. It promised no duration throughout all time for a spiritual soul; it did not look to the gods nor to priests for salvation; it placed no reliance on magic or mere ritual or ecclesiastical organization; it took up into itself the morality of sympathetic love but it did not restrict its vision to the form of this morality; it did not temporize with the existing social structure when this hindered the quest for salvation; it was not based on a cleavage of the natural and the supernatural; it was friendly to the scientific attitude; its common-sense cosmology, vast in sweep, was based on no superscientific system of metaphysics; it purged the essentially religious life of all unessential dross. And in all these respects the new religion is at one with its ancient predecessor. In using the full resources of modern science and of psychology in particular, in bringing to the aid of the individual the instruments of an expanded technology, in seeing the significance of art in the presentation and clarification of the vision of value, in linking itself with the temper of contemporary naturalism, in finding salvation in the attainment of the attitude of generalized detached-attachment, the new religion develops directions implicit in the old.

For these reasons it has seemed fitting to borrow the name of

the predicted Enlightened One. That his name means in San-
skrit "friend" suggests he would not find strange the same
combination of attitudes of attachment and detachment which
friendship itself involves; and the fact that Buddhism under-
went bodhisattva and tantric infiltrations would suggest that
the new turner of the Wheel should not be adverse to a more
specific incorporation of promethean and dionysian traits.

Nevertheless, Maitreyism stands no closer to Buddhism than
it does to other paths of life. A diagram will help make clearer
the relation of the seven paths to each other.

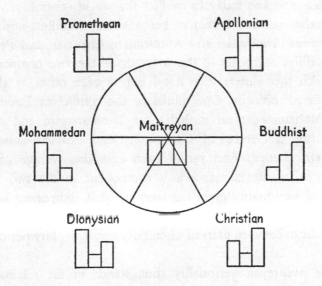

Certain of the types of personality stand in a relation which
might be called that of competitors. Christian and Dionysian,

Apollonian and Buddhist, Mohammedan and Promethean each have one component of personality of the same strength as the other member of the pair, and differ only in the strength of the other two strongly developed components. Thus the Christian and the Dionysian are both weak in the promethean component and both have highly developed dionysian and buddhistic components, but while the former is somewhat stronger in the case of the Dionysian, the latter is somewhat stronger in the Christian. They are brothers under the skin and competitors in the same domain; hence the lure of each for the other and their easy juxtaposition and transformation: Dionysus struggles with Christ in Nietzsche; the Apollonian ideal of man is crossed by that of the Buddhistic contemplative life in Book 10 of Aristotle's *Ethics*; the Mohammedans and Prometheans are locked today in conflict for world control.

Another relation is that of being aliens. Buddhist and Mohammedan, Dionysian and Apollonian, Christian and Promethean differ markedly in the strength of the two components in which they differ: they stand before each other as aliens, difficult to reconcile. One thinks of the conflict of Buddhism and Mohammedanism in India, of Dionysianism and Apollonianism in Greece, of Christianity and Prometheanism in northern Europe. And yet in each case the average of the strengths of the corresponding component in the two alien types of personality gives the strength that component has in the Maitreyan type of personality; in this sense the Maitreyan is the mean between pairs of alien but complementary personalities.

The Maitreyan personality thus stands in the relation of competitor to every other personality, in the relation of alien to none, and as the mean between alien types. No other personality stands in this relation; the Maitreyan is uniquely fitted to understand the other types of personality, to interpret them to each other, and to serve as a hub for a society in which the conflict of personalities could be mitigated without being eradicated.

The same point can be made with respect to the paths of life which the various types of personality have evolved. Each of these paths will seem to the Maitreyan to contain essential wisdom, and yet this wisdom will take on a distinctive character by being incorporated in the Maitreyan attitude.

The Maitreyan will accept Buddhistic detachment—but only within a life strong in attachment to the whole human body; he will welcome Dionysian abandonment—but only when extended to the full release of all human interests and all levels of the self; he will acknowedge Promethean inventiveness—but only when it does not sap delight in the present and in contemplative meditation; he will cherish with the Apollonian the appreciation of cultural achievements—but only if the future is not crucified through adoration of the past and present; he will incorporate the Christian conception of love—but only when it is freed from sentimentality and frustration, and extended to all selves; he will appreciate the outwardly lived strength of conviction of the Mohammedan—but only when conviction has lost its tryannical head and its brute's fist. Each seed of wisdom, in being accepted, is transformed by its inclusion in a dynamic system in which other insights exercise their due control. The resulting attitude of the Maitreyan is no artificial synthesis. It answers to a specific type of personality which stands in a unique relation to other types of personality. It is not compounded of them simply because it can utilize their books of wisdom. Maitreya is a distinct god even though his visage reveals—to the Maitreyan—something of the features of the other gods. If he is something of the Enlightened One, the Lover, the Reveler, the Destroyer, the Maker, and the Conserver, he is none of these alone and completely. If the resulting attitude is complex and subtle, must this not be the case if it is to express the subtlety and complexity of the developed human self?

Because of this complexity, the Maitreyan life is necessarily intense and variegated; its balance can only be a dynamic balance requiring continual flexibility in its maintenance; the range of its attachment requires completion by the nonpossessiveness inherent in detachment. Such a life finds its appropriate expression in the cardinal Maitreyan virtue: Maitreyan friendliness. For to be a friend requires abandonment and restraint, sympathy and severity, frankness and flexibility, challenge and considerateness, giving and withholding. The Maitreyan life is as difficult, as complex, and as vital as the finest friendship.

It is the usual procedure for a religious path of life to buttress itself on a philosophic base which aims to show that the religious attitude and religious goal are grounded "in the nature of things." The form of presentation would often suggest that the philosophy in some sense comes first and that the religion follows from it by implication. But while knowledge may and does influence human attitudes, it is equally true that the dominance of an attitude determines to some degree what is noticed in the world, and in large part how what is noticed is evaluated. Thus there is already in the Buddhist doctrine that life is suffering, a selection of certain features of human experience and an evaluation that suffering is of negative value—a selection and an evaluation quite foreign to, say, a Dionysian temperament. The recognition of this situation makes it impossible for the Maitreyan to say that his way is *the* way; his appeal can only be to human nature, and his marshaling of evidence can mean only the presentation of those statements about the world and man which seem to him true and to make wise the adoption of his own dominant attitude. In so far as he recognizes the existence of types of personality other than his own, he must admit the existence of other paths than his own. But in so far as types of personality are built up out of similar components, what he says may make some appeal to persons other than his own type; and since he himself is distinguished by the presence of all components of personality in a rather high degree, he can act as an interpreter of various individuals to themselves and as a bridge between individuals of different types.

The Maitreyan account of human nature rests on and must be controlled by the scientific studies of man. Subject always to modification by such control, it seems to be true that all men have in varying degrees the need of satisfying their primary biological urges, of living within some form of society, of exercising some sort of constructive manipulation of human and nonhuman objects in their environment, and of attaining some form of rational self-control. These needs differ in intensity and in relative strength in different individuals, and no formula for the conduct of life will fit all cases. It would seem to follow that a society which recognized the existence of all the components of personality and the differences of individuals could best do justice to the diverse problems of its members and utilize most effectively their diverse resources. In so far as the Maitreyan ideal could come to dominance, this kind of society could be actualized without any attempt being made to force each individual into the Maitreyan mold. Such a society would have to provide opportunity for the release of all components of selfhood without expecting that all individuals would or should make equal use of all resources; the presence of the Maitreyan ideal of man would temper the tendencies to excess of any one component of the personality without attempting to obliterate the differences between individuals.

In so far as men have needs in common, these needs would be met from the resources of the community; but beyond this common basis differences of outlook, behavior, and achievement would be expected and encouraged. Such a society would prevent the dominance of types of personality which make impossible the ways of life of other types. It would not erect possessiveness of things or persons into a sanctioned ideal. It would need such institutions as would take account of all clashes of interest; it would have to have a free science ever on the quest for more accurate knowledge; it would utilize to the full the refinements in technique made possible by such knowledge; it would encourage a vigorous art; it would develop an educational orientation which would alike release and train perceptual activities, the manipulation of materials, and the agencies for rational self-control.

The Maitreyan can point to the history of biological organisms for evidence that an integrated social life is compatible with a high order of differentiation among its members; he can summon the biologist to show the interconnections of the functions of the autonomic nervous system, the system of the striped muscles, and the central nervous system—systems respectively active in the dionysian, promethean, and buddhistic components of personality; he can call upon the constitutional psychologist for evidence concerning analysis of types of personality; he can utilize the developments of social psychology to ground his views as to the social context in which individuality develops—so that no blanket opposition of "individual" and "social" is possible; he can call the psychopathologist as witness to the need of some general attitude of orientation which will give integration to the biologically and socially conditioned components of the personality without suppressing completely any of these components.

The history of human culture is a further source of relevant considerations. We have seen the tendency of the historical religions to come in the course of their development under the control of different types of persons and to modify their beliefs and practices in a way to accommodate, at least partially, persons for whom the original path of life was unsatisfactory. This would suggest the possibility of doing deliberately what the special religions have to some degree been forced involuntarily to do. The Maitreyan type of personality has, it is true, as yet received no adequate cultural or religious expression. It may be, however, that this type of person has never had a social environment in which he could come to prominence. A considerable development of mankind is necessary to provide such an elaboration of the various biologically grounded components of the self that they can all find a chance for intense and relatively simultaneous release. Biologically speaking, it has been a difficult task for the human animal to co-ordinate his brain and his hands and his viscera; if social life has on the one hand intensified the task by forcing him to take others into consideration in his action, it has on the other hand so enriched the opportunities for expression that release of brain and hand and viscera are more easily compatible. Today it is at least theoretically possible, and indeed becoming socially necessary, that the release of one personality component utilize the co-operation of the others. In so far, then, as contemporary conditions tend to favor individuals with the release of the Dionysian, the manipulative energy and skill of the Promethean, the objective knowledge and personal control of the Buddhist, and the concern for others of the Christian, they favor the Maitreyan type of personality.

Western society may furnish such a favorable soil for the initiation of the Maitreyan epoch. It embodies a remarkable tension through the diversities of its traditions:—unparalleled technical developments, the highest flights yet attained by the scientific mind, a morality grounded in love and demanding in principle a recognition of the diversities of human individuals, an undercurrent of monasticism and mysticism, a rich earthly sensibility and sensuality. The interpenetration of the Christian and Promethean heritages has prepared Western man for the attitude of detached-attachment. It is true that the Promethean has dominated this culture, and he now leads the struggle against the totalitarianism of a rising Mohammedanism: attachment is the order of the day, not detachment. Yet a number of the ablest persons of this culture have judged this one-sided development of muscle and machines, and found it wanting. "The decline of the West" may mark only the end of Promethean dominance. A victory of the Mohammedans would prolong indefinitely the appearance of a more open and humanely diversified world, but such orgiastic drives have usually spent in time their powers of unification, and the demands for detachment, for love, for leisure to look, for self-direction, for the free interchange of opinion are perforce kept alive in the submerged types of human beings.

It is the fate of the United States to be a major actor in the next act of mankind's play. It is the major threat to the forces which make for a world Mohammedan culture. It is still for the moment a predominantly Promethean culture. From the

Maitreyan perspective it is deficient in a multitude of ways. And yet it might, if it survives, provide the easiest transition to such a culture. It is in principle committed to freedom of religion, of opinion, of the inquiring mind; in principle it is dedicated to take account of the particularities of each individual and permit this individual to attain his maximum development; in principle it is provided with a governmental mechanism by which all clashes of interest are to be objectified and resolved. These principles have by no means been consistently followed, and they may not stand the shock of violent crisis. But they are a bulwark, and they could provide the entrance to a Maitreyan world if Mohammedan world dominance could be forestalled. The physical power of this Promethean land is the best promise that it can be forestalled; if it is, the Maitreyan world will not be at hand, but its possibility will be less remote—for until the possibility of the physical control of the earth by the Mohammedan type of personality is removed, none but this type of personality can be secure on the earth. The future is yet to be made. The near future may indeed belong, as Spengler believed, to the Caesars. For the moment at least the United States, together with England, Russia, and China, stands in the way. If it can be strong enough without and courageous enough within it may yet be the road to a Maitreyan age. If it is not, an India or a China or a Russia may in time assume the task.

Maitreyism is a religion—in a distinctive sense, a religion of religions. It has sought to find the sources of the religious life in man's problem of orientation in a universe stronger than himself, a universe which both supports and frustrates his impulses. Maitreyism understands that different types of personality vary in the strength of needs which they share in common, and differ in their demands for orientation. It respects the various forms which the religious quest has taken; it is tolerant of their differences; it wishes as far as possible to incorporate their germinal impulses in its own wider synthesis. From its point of view the various special religions are diverse emphases, to serve the needs of diverse types of persons in diverse forms of environment, of the same basic factors and impulses which operate in all men and women. If, and as, men's knowledge takes the same form and the technological sources for control spread over the earth, the Maitreyan assumes that men—without denying their differences—will recognize the needs and the agony which they share in common, and that a world religion—a religion of religions, a religion with gifts for all men—will progressively emerge to supplement, though not necessarily to supplant, the local religions. Since the Maitreyan envisages the gods as models projecting the various types of men and the features of the universe to which such men are attentive, he is not intolerant of polytheism and welcomes a pantheon of the gods; and yet, from his point of view the gods of the local religions will seem to him "incarnations," transformations, even distortions, of his own ideal, the man-god, Maitreya. And though he is aware of the human and cosmic sources of the gods, and attentive to their genealogy and necrology, he can still, understanding their nature, live mythologically, drawing upon all the myths in which men have endeavored to concretize themselves and their envisaged universe, and adding to them his own. He too comes to fulfill and not to destroy.

And yet—even a religion of religions is *a* religion. If it appeals to men in so far as they are alike, it will incur the hostility of men in so far as they differ. Maitreyism as a religion competes with other religions, and its votaries are not exempt from struggle. The situation is analogous to that met in the attempt to unify scientific knowledge: even if this is done in the spirit and interest of science itself it encounters something of distrust and hostility from the specialist in the particular sciences, as though he feared that the particularity of his own efforts was thereby endangered. An art which dares to use media previously restricted to particular arts finds itself in the same situation. As a religion, Maitreyism makes its strongest appeal to certain types of persons; though it is open to all, it can expect hostility and distrust from the religions through which other types of persons have projected their ideals. Its tolerance can extend only in so far as it itself is tolerated. Within these limits its tolerance is great: Maitreya is the name of a friendly one. It is not in spirit a religion of the sword. Its path is open to all those whose footgear fits its slope. It has no sanction beyond the impulses of human nature. It addresses itself to the mind of the individual, and through his mind to his particular needs; it does not aim to force itself upon anyone; each individual is free to accept or reject for himself part or whole of the orientation of life which it makes available. But by the same token the Maitreyan must see that his path is available to himself and to others; and in this he defines the limits of his tolerance.

As a religion setting high value on scientific intelligence, Maitreyism will be sympathetic to a scientifically oriented philosophy concerned with the integration of knowledge, and including the relation of such knowledge to other human activities. As a path of life, however, it is based on the acceptance of an attitude—that of generalized detached-attachment; and this in turn arises from its choice of a life as rich in sentiment and in action as in thought. This attitude defines its table of values and provides the goal of its endeavors. It will—in so far as it becomes operative—gradually accumulate techniques by which this attitude can be attained and satisfied. It will develop its own religious literature, its expression in the arts, its ideal of society, its conception of personal relations, its philosophy, its festival of celebration. The roots of Maitreyism lie deep in human nature and in human culture. It is new only in the clarity with which it begins of late to raise itself to consciousness, and in the insistency with which it seeks a fit expression and a fit habitation. Only now does it dare to voice its demands and raise its altar, and offer itself as a religion upon which a new human epoch, a new world culture at once unified and diversified, can be built.

Deep is his love for mankind and sacred he holds its future —but the vision of the votary of Maitreya is not bounded by mankind nor is his dwelling place the future. The salvation he seeks is a quality to be imparted to life while living. It is a quality of life akin to good sportsmanship—the deepest concrete expression which the West has given to the attitude of detached-attachment. The sportsman plays the game for the play itself; he plays to win if possible, but he can meet defeat; he plays vigorously and he deals strong blows, but his action is friendly and he has the delight of a spectator to his own sport. In the cosmic game man is but a player. The Maitreyan has regained the vast Indian vision of Nitya Lila—the sport of the gods. He has joined in the sport. He mixes freely in the divine play, knowing that the game outlives him as it outlives the gods he and the universe together engender. His eyes are clear for the exuberant tumult of the Great Festival, and his ears have heard the drumbeats of the Days and Nights of Brahma. At home everywhere, needing no home anywhere; mixed with all and hovering over all; aware of the dawns which follow midnights, and the midnights which gather the harvest sown in the dawns and ripened in the days—such are the sources of his solemnity, his agony, his peace, his vision, his abandonment, his activity, and his joy.

VIII. The Living God

"It is a fearful thing to fall into the hands of the living God."

Hebrews 10:31

"There will be a new man, happy and proud. For whom it will be the same to live or not to live, he will be the new man. He who will conquer pain and terror will himself be a god. . . . No, not in a future eternal life, but in eternal life here. There are moments, you reach moments, and time suddenly stands still. . . . He will come, and his name will be the man-God."

Kirillov, in Dostoievski's *The Possessed*

"Why do you not think of him as the coming one, immiment from all eternity, the future one, the final fruit of a tree whose leaves we are? What keeps you from projecting his birth into coming ages and living your life like a painful and beautiful day in the history of a great gestation? Do you not see, how everything that happens is always beginning again, and could it not be *his* beginning, since beginning in itself is always so beautiful? If he is the most perfect, must not the lesser be *before* him, so that he can select himself out of fullness and overflow? —Must he not be the last, in order to include everything in himself, and what sense would we have if he, whom we long for, had already been?"

Rilke:
Letters to a Young Poet

VIII

The Living God

SUCH are seven ways—it is believed the seven major ways—in which men have given a direction to their lives and an integration to their multifarious and competing interests. Each is in essentials the attainment of a dominant attitude (an apical interest) in terms of which all other interests are regulated. The religious individual is described in terms of the attitude which in fact characterizes his life or to which he gives his allegiance —and these two, though interrelated, are by no means the same. The individual, in virtue of his biological disposition, is inclined toward one or another of these paths of life, and in some cases he may attain the congenial path without great difficulty. But in other cases this may not be so: conflicts among the components of his personality may cause him, temporarily at least, to give his allegiance to a mode of life which promises release from his conflict, as when the Buddhistic ideal offers itself as a refuge from the storm of dionysian indulgence. These are the dramatic moments of "conversion," moments which may indicate a permanent reorientation of an entire life, or which may be merely a passing phase in the struggle of the individual for an as yet unattained (and perhaps never to be attained) integration. The strenuous advocacy of a particular path of life is itself a sign that the individual is seeking this path of life and not merely following it. It is everywhere necessary to distinguish the personality which an individual holds before himself as an ideal and the person which he himself is at the moment. It is equally necessary to distinguish the ideal striven for and the means used to seek its attainment: a person who has given the Buddhistic ideal his allegiance may in fact act as a Promethean in attempting to mold himself and others into the pattern of this ideal. The religious prophet may not be simply expressing his present self in the type of person he advocates, and those who "put the religion over" may themselves be very different persons from the type to which they have given their support.

The paths of life, then, correspond to the lives of certain ideal types of persons, types which are an idealization of the actual personalities of struggling men and women, expressive both of what they are and the directions in which they are moving. These types are given a formulation and a leverage on life by being cast in the symbolism of mythology and religion. So cast, they furnish a pictorial representation of preferred types of men and women, and a model by which living men and women attempt to pattern their lives. They are expressive of human tendencies and longings; their function is an orientational one and not, when properly understood, that of giving an account of external nature which rivals the one furnished by science. This does not mean, of course, that there is no reference to the universe in such symbols: persons inhabit an environment, and what is discerned as environment depends on the person in question. The Dionysian, torn between tendencies to detachment and the tug of stronger biological impulses, lets himself go explosively when detachment is overcome; he is keenly aware of suffering, struggle, the destructive power of elemental forces, and the joy in the release of such forces. Siva is one of the models projected by the Dionysian temperament: it is fitting that he is seen both as the great ascetic and as the great destroyer; he is presented as the destroyer of Kama, the goddess of sexual love; the chain of skulls which he wears around his neck attests the trophies of death; his symbol, the phallus, and the vanquished corpse upon which he sits signalize the release and the joy of life's eternal renewal. There are, of course, destructive and generative processes in the wider universe just as there are in the life of man which is part of this universe. The Dionysian is peculiarly attentive to such processes, and the figure of Siva incorporates at once features of human life and the wider universe. This reference to the world may be distilled out and stated as scientific truths about man and nature, but such reference is by no means the sole element of the Siva symbol and no substitute for the task of descriptive science: the symbol is primarily an expression of the tendency of a certain type of temperament to see the world in a certain light, and a device by which such a person gives effective integration and orientation to his own activities.

It is a shallow, though a natural, tendency for the person addicted to science to scorn religious symbols (such as 'God'), and to talk with Freud of the end of an "illusion," as though description of the world and the prediction of its course were the only legitimate functions of signs. It is true that this is a healthy counteraction to the frequent tendency of the religionist to talk as if religious utterances were rivals to scientific knowledge of the world—but one shallowness need not engender a second. Once the essentially expressive and orientational aspect of religious symbolism is recognized (so that 'God' is seen as the key symbol which men have used to express the preferred type of personality to which their own orientation tends), the deeper task becomes that of interpreting how past religious symbols have functioned and of finding signs which the individual of today can use in expressing his own longings and in giving to his own life a sense of direction. This need is inherent in life; if persons sympathetic to science cannot perform this function, or at least see the need of its performance in ways which do not negate science in its own sphere, then they can be sure that other types of persons will do this task in their own way,—and the world which results may not be a world in which the scientific attitude is accorded a high place.

The task of the orientation of contemporary men and women is the task of contemporary religion. The forces operative in this task are the voice of the living God. If the historic forms of religion prove inacceptable—and certainly to a very large number of persons they are inacceptable—then a new religion will emerge. Psychologically expressed, this means that contemporary men are struggling to attain a symbolism by which they can picture a type of person whom they take as the ideal to which they themselves can effectively strive; religiously expressed, this means that a new god is struggling for birth. Fearful it is indeed to fall into the hands of this living God; more fearful it is, as D. H. Lawrence has said, "to fall out of them"!

Since the dominant attitude of an individual controls the expression of every subordinate interest of the individual, each major type of personality expresses itself in a characteristic form of philosophy, art, and society. Each has its own system of valuation, so that even where the same term is used by different types of persons to refer to the same cultural fact (and this is by no means always the case), the evaluation of the phenomena will differ: 'love,' 'reason,' 'human nature,' 'science,' 'art,' 'morality,' and the like will either refer to different phenomena or will express different attitudes toward and evaluations of the same phenomena. Thus each type of person will regard as "good" that which satisfies the hierarchized set of interests reflected in the type of person which he is or which he tries to be; each type will then have its own "morality," or if the term 'morality' be given a specific uniform reference, each type will assign to morality a different place in its system of values. Thus the Dionysian will refuse to recognize the Christian morality as his own morality, or if he consents to designate by 'morality' what the Christian designates by the term, he will oppose such morality; the Mohammedan on the other hand, if he accepts the Christian use of 'morality,' will confine the range of application of the term to members of his own faith; the Buddhist, with his eye set on individual salvation, will utilize, but in the end pass beyond, "good and evil" when these are conceived in social terms. Or, to take another example, the Dionysian "going along" with the world will be inclined to a philosophy which is affirmative in tone and which recognizes chance and caprice in the world; the Buddhist, bent on attaining salvation through his own efforts, will be "pessimistic" as to the course of natural existence and will find in himself the source for his troubles, blaming his attitude in this life, or if that is not sufficient, his attitude in previous lives; the Promethean, dedicated to molding the world to his heart's desire, will be both "mechanistic" and "free-willist" in attitude, believing alike in the "laws" which express the obdurate nature of his material and his ability to transform this matter in terms of his goals, and in the possibility that things will "come out all right" if only he himself is zealous·enough. Similarly, the conflicts about "romantic" and "classical" art, about "impressionistic" and "abstract" art, show themselves under analysis to go back to the clash of types of personalities and their corresponding systems of evaluations.

Such indications are at best suggestive; this is not the occa-

sion to give a comprehensive comparison of the cultural implications of the various dominant attitudes which characterize the
major types of personality. But one point—though it cannot be
sufficiently developed—must be brought to the forefront of
attention: the relation of types of personality to types of society.
In recent decades the attention to society has drawn attention
away from noticing the peculiarities of the individual. We have
noticed that this emphasis is now happily changing—happily
unless it in turn neglects what has already been gained, for
wisdom in these matters requires that we no longer operate in
terms of a careless opposition of "individual" and "society."

A thing gets whatever characteristics it has within some system of things of which it is a member. But having got them,
they in turn influence the properties it will show when it becomes a member of another system. The opposition is never a
wholesale opposition of what a thing is "in itself" and what it
is because of contact with other things: all such oppositions
as "heredity and environment," "constitutional nature and
social environment," "individual and society" refer merely to
the distinction between what something is in one system and
what then happens to it when placed in another system. With
this understanding, it may be said that an individual at birth
has a tendency toward a certain type of personality, but that
what he becomes will be in part influenced by the "society" into
which he is born. Now this society is itself, in turn, composed
of individuals whose personality is a function both of their
"constitutional nature" and the society in which they developed
—there is no general opposition of "individual" and "society,"
nor contradiction in saying both that society influences the
individual and the individual influences the society. The society
of any one time is in fact nothing but an interrelated system

of individuals whose natures were themselves in part determined by the earlier society in which they matured.

The characteristic feature of a society at any time is to be found in the prominence of the roles which various types of individuals perform. In so far as a particular type of individual dominates the culture, the society will itself reflect the activities and evaluations of such individuals: it can then be characterized, for example, as an Apollonian or a Dionysian society. In so far as no one type dominates the culture, the society is more or less "polytheistic." Where one type is dominant or a number of types share a preferred status, other types of persons will fit into the scheme as best they can, giving to the conventional rites and phrases something of their own interpretation, but always constituting something of a threat in case the existing path of society permits them to seek in some degree a more congenial mode of life. Seen from this point of view, the dynamics of social change within a society and between societies is to be looked for (at least in part) in the conditions which give to certain types of personality a preferred status. There seems to be here a kind of social "wheel of the law" (represented in the previous diagram) which needs to be more carefully stated and studied than can now be done, but which sheds considerable light on the situation of contemporary man.

Let us suppose a society essentially Apollonian. Such a society is dominated by the ideals of an active socially oriented personality, loyal to the achievements of the society and detached enough from activity to be able to render them conscious homage; moderation, civic virtues, a serenity anchored in the present will be esteemed; the Promethean innovator and the demonic Dionysian and the withdrawing Buddhist will all be condemned. Nevertheless, the Dionysians and the Buddhists will fare better than the extreme Promethean, for they do not work by getting control of the physical resources of the culture, and may even pay lip service to that culture. They are, however, inwardly hostile to the Apollonian view, and the more this culture becomes stereotyped, the more they tend to withdraw and seek the companionship of kindred selves. Persons of the Christian type, finding no adequate social outlet for their temperament, tend to band together in a similar way. This withdrawal itself weakens the structure of the society. The dominant groups in turn become more reactionary and more fearsome, and cling tenaciously to formulae and techniques no longer adequate to the problems posed within the group and through contacts with other groups. The demands for a way of life become more insistent for all types of persons.

Under such circumstances the Mohammedans have their chance. As men of action and strong feeling, high in both the dionysian and promethean components, they show decision, and by use of force and emotionality give the group a sense of direction. The Apollonians and Dionysians follow along, although the pace is rather violent for individuals with such high buddhist components (better a book or a bed! they may say to themselves in quiet); the Christians and Buddhists are simply pushed to one side. The Promethean, however, comes more into his own under the Mohammedan shadow: his technological resources are needed; gradually he transforms the basis of the culture and may become in actuality the dominant type of person. The pace he sets, however, is still a fast one, and the unceasing transformation of the society which his dominance imposes is unsatisfactory to any other type of individual. Resistances develop and his own transforming activity becomes more difficult. All the paths of life now again become clamorous. It is under this situation that Maitreyism and a Maitreyan society might come to dominance, since its attitude does considerable justice to all components of the self and would under such circumstances make some appeal to each of the other types of personality by offering them a society more congenial than that which they could offer to each other. Nevertheless, the situation would be precarious and only under rare conditions could this type of society long continue, since individuals of a stronger promethean component would incline to take control of existing institutions and material goods: the possessive Apollonian type of man will at this point step in, freeze and bless the existing social arrangement. And the wheel begins to turn once more.

How widely this scheme for the dynamics of social development (and possibly also for the development of the individual, as seems to be suggested in the *Faust*) is generally true cannot be our present problem. It has the initial advantage at least that it can make intelligible the type of cultural comparisons which Spengler in *The Decline of the West* has instituted (and his characterizations of the Apollonian, Promethean [Faustian], and Mohammedan [Magian] cultures are rich in insight) without forcing us back to an uneasily locatable "soul" of the culture and without making it impossible for the same geographical region of the earth to support in turn a number of cultures. The scheme does seem to fit the general development of European culture, and gives a basis for seeing in what sense we are at the end of a cultural epoch and in what sense we may be at the beginning of another.

Put crudely, and beginning for illustration with the Apollonian stage of Greek culture which is given philosophic expression in Plato and Aristotle, the cycle seems to run as follows: As the Apollonian-dominated culture loses its vitality and begins to draw around itself the remnant of its vestments, the buddhistically inclined Stoicism and the mildly dionysian Epicureanism evidence the social withdrawal of types of persons to whom the older culture was personally unsatisfactory. In the same stream is the growing power of the Dionysian cults, which progressively challenge the supremacy of Apollo, and the spread of the Hellenistic (Dionysian) version of Christianity. The Mohammedan Romans give a protective shell to the culture, and the still more Mohammedan barbarians take in turn the reins of control. Within this shell Mohammedan Christianity works, giving to numerous individuals the pattern of the life of Christ while utilizing the promethean energies of those who at least professed the Christian ideal to extend the power of the Church. Also within this shell the energies of the Promethean type of man were liberated; they noticeably marked the culture of the Italian Renaissance. There is even in this culture—with its joint concern for the body, for art, and for technology—a trace of the Maitreyan element, best embodied in Leonardo da Vinci, artist, scientist, engineer, at once detached and attached.

But a new Apollonianism set in, consecrating the existing cultural attainments. Against this background the cycle again continues: buddhistic individuals sought withdrawal in the monastic life; the Protestant Reformation sought to renew Christ's ideal of life. The "Mohammedan" monarchs imposed their wills upon whomever they could. They needed the Promethean technologist; and under their protection he grew so strong that in the Enlightenment the typical Promethean culture of Western Europe became dominant, believing to have found in a scientifically oriented technology, the political machinery of representative government, and the agency of universal education the means by which men could continually and progressively modify their lives to the ever fuller satisfaction of their desires. The Apollonian settled down to the new situation, blessed it—and took control of the means to retain the world in his conservative image.

We live in the backwash of that situation. In the strict sense of the term we are (and to this extent Spengler's voice is only one of a hundred voices) at the end of a period in which the Promethean voice was the clear voice of the culture. We are in a highly "polytheistic" interim in which—as we shall soon see —every one of the major paths of life is pressing for acceptance. Both the dionysian and the buddhistic components of personality are making their claims against the dominance which has been given in recent centuries to the promethean component. Men of many types and from many points of view have assessed contemporary culture and found it wanting. The struggle to define the type of man who is to be given preferred status in our culture, and his relation to other types of man— and therefore to define ultimately the form of society—is the content of the new religiosity.

That the situation is a difficult one for many persons, that we are in the midst of cultural changes which may determine indefinitely the direction of human history, is certain. But still the question must be asked, in what sense is Spengler correct in calling it a decline? To say merely that we are in the "old age" of a culture is irrelevant unless it is assumed that cultural cycles cannot repeat themselves on old soil (for the end of one cultural period might then mark the beginning of a new one), and in Western society we have seen some evidence that this assumption is questionable. A period in which one cycle is ending and another beginning would be a period of "decline" only for one whose preferred type of personality was expressed in the form of society now becoming obsolete: it would equally well be a "new beginning" for one who thought that his preferred type of personality was coming into its own. Spengler has been insistent on the relation of a "morality" or system of values to a culture; if we see that a society is characterized by the place it assigns to different types of individuals, it follows that vague statements about the decline of a "soul" of a culture must be translated into concrete terms of the type of personality preferred by the person who makes the judgment. I hazard the view that Spengler was himself an Apollonian in temperament, that he without warrant erected into a norm the achievements Western Promethean man had obtained at the Enlightenment, and turned to the Mohammedan to protect such of those achievements as yet remained. There is no evidence for (nor, I believe, meaning, to) the general statement that the West is in a period of decline; from the standpoint of certain types of personality this statement can be made; from the standpoint of others it cannot. To talk of decline in general is merely to confuse the issue, and invoke the sense of doom.

The actual situation is simply that many persons have found the existing society unsatisfactory, and that this society is in a rapid process of change. Their task is to decide on the type of person they themselves wish to be and on the type of persons they wish to see dominant in the society of the future; and to find as far as possible a way of life adequate to their own nature and helpful in bringing about a society in which their chosen type of person will be preferred. This task and such decisions can be framed in the light of the best knowledge available as to the chance of one or another type of person coming to power in the present situation, but no knowledge can take the place of this decision or the energies needed in an attempt to fulfill the task. The making of this decision and the assumption of this task is the living focus of the religious life.

That all the characteristic paths of life bid for the allegiance of living men and women, and that the urge to a new religiosity is insistent, is nowhere more evident than in the art of this period. It is the essential trait of the artist to give sensible habitation to the values to which his own nature is sensitive, so that the domain of art provides an unrivaled source for tracking down the needs and struggles and aspirations of the members of a human community. An adequate use of these sources is not possible in these pages, but even a glance helps to make concrete the factors relevant to the decision which confronts a person alive to contemporary urgencies.

The voice of Dionysus, demanding life intensified by the primitive passions and impulses which a Promethean-Christian culture has endeavored to tame, is unmistakable. It expresses itself in a revolt against the evaluation of life in terms of material comfort, technical efficiency, intellectual detachment, the sentiment of kindliness: it manifests itself in a cult of the primitive, the irrational, the fantastic; it explores with zest all that is conventionally prohibited and condemned—lust, passion, cruelty, conflict, death; it seeks the intensification of life through abandonment, pain, sin. Blake is a protest against the Apollonian Enlightenment; Balzac and Zola turned back the skin of this civilization so that its entrails were visible; Schopenhauer laid bare the impulsive sources of life; Nietzsche justified philosophically the Dionysian cravings; Freud brought the weight of science to exhibit the continued power in the personality of desires rooted in man's biological heritage; the artists have explored with fervor, with pain, with love, this human country of the damned. Baudelaire, seeing "the city as from a tower, hospital, brothel, prison and such hells, where evil comes up softly like a flower" chants to this city—and to Satan "patron of my pain"—:

> I love thee, infamous city! Harlots and
> Hunted have pleasures of their own to give,
> The vulgar herd can never understand.

Rimbaud pulls out from the accepted social structure: he rejects the cult of reason, of science, of progress, of the accepted morality, and the role which this society assigns to art; he supplements the statement "I have never been a Christian!" with the exclamation "Pagan blood returns!" D. H. Lawrence, revolting against cities, the masses, modern technology, seeks renewal of "quickness" in "holy silence" and the mystic rites of sex; "faked love," he writes, "has rotted our marrow"; he predicts that Lucifer's turn is now coming. Jeffers' revolt is similar; but his Dionysianism takes a more cosmic form: tragedy, desire, the "fence vaulter science," "wild love"—these are the forces which break "the mold of humanity"; released from man, "falling in love outward," one obtains surcease from the human agony through contemplation of the awesome purposeless majesty of the cosmic festival. The whole surrealist movement in art is a Dionysian protest against the established art forms, and an attempt to recover what Dali calls the "vital constants" of "love, death, and the perception of space"; its dismemberment of the traditional combination of aesthetic elements, and their recombination in strange forms, is a deliberate attempt to shock the perceptual apparatus into a fresh intensity, to revitalize the sense of the irrational, the mythical, the primitive, the "unconscious."

And yet in all these cases, the Dionysian revolt is not merely a protest: it is often the search for a life of religious intensity. Blake sought for a new marriage of "heaven and hell"; Nietzsche hoped to lay the foundation for a noble tragic era; the dying Baudelaire seeks a new regime of work, sobriety, trust in God: "Man is an animal of worship, to worship is to sacrifice oneself and to prostitute oneself"; Rimbaud "waits for God like a gourmand": "Let us accept every influx of vigor and real tenderness. And, at dawn, armed with an ardent patience we shall enter the splendid cities"; Lawrence writes that unless in place of the old religions a new religion is found "that will connect men with the universe, they will perish"; Jeffers, seeking salvation beyond man in the vision of the terrible beauty of the universe-God, yet hints of a return to man: he feels himself on the gate-sill of the "hawk's dream future," and the women of his poems, refusing to be fugitives from God, take upon themselves the agonized burden of a tortured God's existence: Gudrun affirms, "I will enter the cloud of stars. I will eat the whole serpent again."

The spirit of Prometheus has been confused by the contemporary clamor, but has not abdicated. Where the overt deed has been blocked, it has often remained as an attitude: a refusal to bow one's head before pain or the presentiment of defeat, and an insistence to still do whatever is in one's power. There is something of this attitude of Promethean defiance in Andreyev's *Life of Man*, and in Russell's *A Free Man's Worship*, where the "free man," cognizant of the precariousness of his cosmic position, joins his forces with those of other men,

proudly defiant of the irresistible forces that tolerate, for a moment, his knowledge and his condemnation, to sustain alone, a weary but unyielding Atlas, the world that his own ideals have fashioned despite the trampling march of unconscious power.

Leopardi, distrustful of science and technology, seemed to believe that it is the function of the poet to revivify and direct human life. Others too have expressed this hope for art. Van Gogh, accepting struggle, fighting resignation, finds strength in love conceived as an activity and not as a feeling: Gethsemane is more beautiful than Paradise, Prometheus is given precedence over Jupiter. The constructivists in art, abjuring both subjectivism and representationism, are molding material in an essentially Promethean spirit; and behind their activity is often the hope that such an art will help to revivify the Promethean attitude in the whole domain of life. Nietzsche's Zarathustra, thinking of the philosopher-sage as the creator of values, finally comes down from his buddhistic and dionysian mountain peaks to do his work in the world of man ("Do I seek after my happiness? I seek after my work!"). Marx is likewise in impulse a Promethean figure, working like Nietzsche upon mankind as material to be molded. In the America of Whitman the Promethean attitude is still less confused by the presence of effective rivals. American pragmatism as formulated in James, Dewey, and Mead is infused with this attitude, it permeates the novels of Thomas Wolfe, and its dominance in the national life, as represented by Roosevelt, is still for the moment unquestionable.

In the present babel of the clash of attitudes to dominate life, it is natural that the Mohammedan temperament is insurgent—indeed, even those whose ultimate goal is other than this tend themselves to become Mohammedan to fortify their confidence and to use the service of other Mohammedans to achieve their ends. In the shadow of Nietzsche there stand a Hitler, a Goering, and a Mussolini; behind Marx there arise a

Lenin and a Stalin. The dionysian release of this type of person frees the promethean component to use whatever means are available,—and jeopardizes the existence of every other type of person and mode of life.

It is not merely the Releasers, dominated by the dionysian or promethean components of personality, whose voices are heard today; the Restrainers, in whom the buddhistic components are strong, are equally insistent. Buddhism, recognized as such, is naturally not yet so prominent in the West, though Buddhistic centers have for some time begun to make their appearance in London, Berlin, and even the United States. For the most part the doctrine and attitude is expressed in forms more congenial to the West: there is a subterranean but persistent influence of Spinoza, Schopenhauer, and the tradition of Stoicism; and many buddhistic natures obtain some satisfaction in the detachment which science and art make possible and require. The revival of Buddhistic ideals is often (as in Aldous Huxley) directed to such specific purposes as the weakening of the appeal of modern versions of totalitarian Mohammedanism by calling the individual back to himself as his center. But whatever the motivation, the soil is prepared, and it may safely be predicted that Buddhism—especially in its early form and perhaps in linkage with early Christianity—is destined to have a continually growing influence in the contemporary world. The power which Gandhi has wielded shows the vitality, even in political spheres, of a doctrine which challenges force by restraint and love.

For the most part the reaction against Promethean and Mohammedan dominance in the West aligns itself with the figure

of Christ. Dostoievski's novels present in ever-different forms
the quest of God-hungry men and women for a revitalization
of the Christ ideal; the theme is always the same: "the secret of
man's being is not only to live but to have something to live
for." All of the paths of life are exemplified in these novels,
but the movement, if not the precise form of the answer, is in
one direction: it is away from sensualism, self-assertion, the
will to power, and acquiescence in present society, toward the
image of Christ; the path leads through suffering and expiation
and humility to a life centered inwardly in self-integrity and
turned outward by the force of a purified and universalized
love; the source of stimulus for the new life comes in Dostoievski through the inspiration of some figure in the Church
(in, but hardly of, the present Church) or through some
humble prostitute whose submission to lust has only served to
intensify a love whose integrity and strength would have been
more visible to Christ than to those who appropriate her body.
Tolstoy's writings are a more tortured and less convincing
exhibition of the turn away from a world of Dionysians, Prometheans, Apollonians, and Mohammedans to a Buddhistic-
Christian outlook based on faith, sympathetic love, work, and
human brotherhood, and on a repudiation of anger, property,
and the nationalist state. Rilke, for all his dionysian tendencies,
has perhaps presented in the noblest and purest and most utilizable form the living residuum of the Christian heritage of love.
Rejecting alike the feverish external activity of the Promethean,
the emotionally desensitizing withdrawal of the Buddhist, and
the sentimentality by which Christian sentiment is endangered, Rilke's life was a search for integrity, for self-purification, for self-intensification. And the elemental themes of love
and death and beauty and the quest for God stand forth again
with depth and clarity. His religious search—like that of

Dostoievski and Tolstoy—is the search for a life filled and
directed by love, so that the eye may again see cleanly and man
again may praise; like Christ he views religion as a direction
of the heart; and in finding this direction for himself he un-
covered strata and significances of love which contemporary man
seeks with hunger, and whose possibility he had long since
begun to doubt.

The Apollonian man, ill at ease in a swiftly flowing culture,
tries to single out some form of the cultural heritage which
seems to embody high human achievements to be preserved. In
the West that means for the most part an attempt to link together in some way the humanistic traditions of classical Greece
with the institution of the Christian Church. T. S. Eliot and
Jacques Maritain signalize this tendency. Since Aquinas had
already attempted a linkage of Christian and Aristotelian Apollonianism, he (or Aristotle alone) has provided for the contemporary Apollonian a possible rallying point more effective
for many persons than, say, Santayana's naturalistic version of
Aristotle. The Catholic Church has—perhaps fatally—rested
its case on Aquinas, and the path to the ark of this Church
is well worn by the shoes of men and women seeking stability.
For while the Church is in one sense "anti-modern," its social
ideals provide shelter for social aspirations frustrated in the
capitalist world, its stress on the individual offers some hope
of preserving the related democratic stress on the individual
which the totalitarian regimes deny, its separation of reason
and revelation gives considerable play for the type of detached
investigation needed in science, and its institutional strength
seems to provide a bulwark to the Apollonian mind against
the onslaught of—to it—alien and insurgent personalities. The
result is a real, if somewhat plaintive and even frantic, hope
that by clinging to the raft of the Great Tradition—by reading

the great classics of literature and philosophy, by joining the Church or at least advancing its purposes—the already attained wisdom and institutions of Western man will provide guidance to the individual and a center of resistance to an upset "such as the world has never seen before," which was predicted by Dostoievski and many sensitive individuals of this era. Contemporary Protestantism, equally ill at ease as a result of its union of Christian and Promethean motives, and lacking doctrinal and institutional cohesion, is fluid and uncertain in direction; Neo-scholasticism is Apollonian and conservative in tendency, and its temptation will be to give its oracular blessing to whatever social order wins out, provided that it is permitted to interpret these results in terms of its ancient symbols and slogans. Christianity still stands Janus-faced.

The Maitreyan has received no such definite expression in the contemporary world as have the celebrants of the other ways, and where his figure does appear it is as yet partly clothed in more familiar masks and names. The attitude of detached-attachment is frequently suggested, but in a partial rather than generalized form: some component of personality does not receive its due, or the preference is weighted toward either the more elementary biological manifestation of these components or the more complex manifestation which an involved social development has given them.

The suggestions which come from the poets often fail to do justice to the promethean side of this type of man, in turning against the intricate net of modern technology, and in erecting the promethean demands into an attitude unsupported by the contact with the materials which it needs for its nourishment.

This is the case with Leopardi, with Rilke, with Jeffers. In their poems the Maitreyan will recognize his search for the attitude of detached-attachment, but something is missing: the linkage of this attitude with the material problems and resources of the day. These men have fortified themselves; they have cleansed their perception, their thoughts, their emotions for a new task; they feel themselves at the door of a significant future—but their hand grasps only the pen and their feet turn only to the rooms of their retreat. Take, for example, Jeffers' proposed symbol in *Rock and Hawk*:

> Here is a symbol in which
> Many high tragic thoughts
> Watch their own eyes.
>
> This gray rock, standing tall
> On the headland, where the seawind
> Lets no tree grow,
>
> Earthquake-proved, and signatured
> By ages of storms: on its peak
> A falcon has perched.
>
> I think, here is your emblem
> To hang in the future sky;
> Not the cross, not the hive,
>
> But this; bright power,.dark peace;
> Fierce consciousness joined with final
> Disinterestedness;
>
> Life with calm death; the falcon's
> Realist eyes and act
> Married to the massive

Mysticism of stone,
Which failure cannot cast down
Nor success make proud.

Here is the attachment, the courage, the tension of the hawk;
the imperturbability, the coldness, the endurance of granite:—
but neither the hawk nor the stone knows love of man or machine, nor can hawk's talons or rock's surface stop or direct
a machine-dominated world. Leopardi's *Ginestra* has alike
transcended defiance and groveling and self-immolation—but
its fruits are scattered on a desert. The World War brought
Rilke face to face with forces which he could not understand,
and paralyzed his own creativity until he had sunk again for
nourishment into the deepest recesses of himself.

Nietzsche's superman was the attempt to set before man an
ideal which would liberate and direct him through an age of
nihilism. And yet how vague, how susceptible to diverse in-
terpretations it is! Zarathustra revels before the universe as a
Dionysian celebrant, meditates on his mountain heights as an
anchorite, descends to the world of man to accomplish his work.
He is dionysian, buddhistic, promethean—and yet no pattern
emerges with clarity. We are left with his resolve to work
among men; but how he will work and with what instruments
and to what end remains in doubt. Nietzsche tries to seduce us
with a type of man (*that* is the key to this most complex and
baffling of modern personalities), but the outlines of the type
are vague. There is in Nietzsche a disdain for the entire realm
of technology which could anchor the promethean surge of
his projected superman; he is left with the tension of a dynamic
life, but a tension whose outlet is not indicated. There are
only vague references to "work," to "war," to "blond beasts,"
to Napoleonic "half-gods half-men,"—and the bare intimations

of the Maitreyan type of man have been distorted by the Mohammedans to their own ends.

The reverse of this situation is found in those persons in whom the promethean component is dominant, and yet who adumbrate an image of man which transcends the Promethean type. The Communist has caught sight of energetic and expansive men and women who could utilize the machine within a life leisurely enough to permit the detachment of science and art—but the image was blurred, and with verbal obeisance to the "classless society," the Mohammedans could—as in the case of the utilizers of Nietzsche—fill in this vague image in terms of themselves. Dewey's development is instructive in this connection. His later writings show an increasing recognition of, and sense of intimacy with, the naturalistically conceived cosmos in which man acts. And yet, taking his writings as a whole, the promethean emphasis is dominant and in danger of forcing every other phase of human culture and activity to its service as its "instrument"; the result is that the suggestions of a Maitreyan conception of the self are forced into the background by an essentially Promethean emphasis, so that many types of persons fail to find in Dewey an expression of motives essential to their own nature.

Thomas Mann's *The Magic Mountain* is a vivid dramatization of contemporary man's search for a way of life. Hans Castorp is forced by chance and tuberculosis and inertia to postpone his career as an engineer in the workaday flat-land world. The mountain sanatorium requires withdrawal and detachment, and permits him to clarify his nature and goal through contact with the various personalities whose lives impinge on his. There he meets the detached objectivity of the scientific outlook, and through Clavdia the release of the dionysian primitive impulses ("Passion, that is self-forgetfulness"). But these are but incidental to his clash with the main forces which in fact dominate this day: the clash between the Promethean Settembrini and the Mohammedan Naphta. Settembrini is the Promethean spirit which has already begun to compromise with Apollo: there is something heroic in his attempt to wipe out human suffering through the rational and social control of nature and human society; something emotionally barren in the hostility of his intellect to the "mystical" and "evil" forces of nature's dance of love and death; something pathetic in the reluctant recognition of the strength of forces opposing his humanitarian ideal, so that he must fight though opposing physical power as such. In Naphta the main contemporary anti-Promethean forces converge to a Mohammedan focus: the dominance of the spirit of "bourgeois" Enlightenment is seen as the degradation of humanity; there is a Dionysian acceptance of death and suffering and the weakness of the flesh; the buddhistic aspect of personality is to be satisfied by "discipline, sacrifice, renunciation of the ego, the curbing of the personality"; the Church and the proletariat are to unite against the falling bourgeois order in the coming reign of Terror, and to destroy the state, the family, secular art, and science by a Communistic ideal. Yet there are discords in this self: Settembrini correctly notes that at heart Naphta is a "voluptuary," and in the duel, Naphta, unable to summon himself to the terroristic deed, shoots himself instead of Settembrini.

Hans Castorp is influenced by both Settembrini and Naphta, but the position to which he struggles agrees with neither. The language in which he expresses his forming attitude is clothed in a Christianized Promethean dress (an evidence that the new attitude has not yet created its own symbols), but the content of his utterance shows an attempt to combine somehow the dionysian, promethean, and buddhistic sides of human nature into an attitude which unites the strength of detachment to the strength of attachment:

I have dreamed of man's state, of his courteous and enlightened social state; behind which, in the temple, the horrible blood-sacrifice was consummated. Were they, those children of the sun, so sweetly courteous to each other, in silent recognition of that horror? It would be a fine and right conclusion they drew. I will hold to them, in my soul, I will hold with them and not with Naphta, neither with Settembrini. They are both talkers; the one luxurious and spiteful, the other for ever blowing on his penny pipe of reason, even vainly imagining he can bring the mad to their senses. It is all Philistinism and morality, most certainly it is irreligious. Nor am I for little Naphta either, or his religion, that is only a *guazzabuglio* of God and the Devil, good and evil, to the end that the individual soul shall plump into it head first, for the sake of mystic immersion in the universal. Pedagogues both! Their quarrels and counter-positions are just a *guazzabuglio* too, and a confused noise of battle, which need trouble nobody who keeps a little clear in his head and pious in his heart. Their aristocratic question! Disease, health! Spirit, nature! Are those contradictions? I ask, are they problems? No, they are no problems, neither is the problem of their aristocracy. The recklessness of death is in life, it would not be life without it—and in the centre is the position of the *Homo Dei*, between recklessness and reason, as his state is between mystic community and windy individualism. I, from my column, perceive all this. In this state he must live gallantly, associate in friendly reverence with himself, for only he is aristocratic, and the counter-positions are not at all. Man is the lord of counter-positions, they can be only through him, and thus he is more aristocratic than they. More so than death, too aristocratic for death—that is the freedom of his mind. More aristocratic than life, too aristocratic for life, and that is the piety in his heart.

There is both rhyme and reason in what I say, I have made a dream poem of humanity. I will cling to it. I will be good. I will let death have no mastery over my thoughts. For therein lies goodness and love of humankind, and in nothing else. Death is a great power. One takes off one's hat before him, and goes weavingly on tiptoe. He wears the stately ruff of the departed and we do him honour in solemn black. Reason stands simple before him, for reason is only virtue, while death is release, immensity, abandon, desire. Desire, says my dream. Lust, not love. Death and love—no, I cannot make a poem of them, they don't go together. Love stands opposed to death. Only love, not reason, gives sweet thoughts. And from love and sweetness alone can form come: form and civilization, friendly, enlightened, beautiful human intercourse—always in silent recognition of the blood-sacrifice. Ah, yes, it is well and truly dreamed. I have taken stock. I will remember. I will keep faith with death in my heart, yet well remember that faith with death and the dead is evil, is hostile to humankind, so soon as we give it power over thought and action. *For the sake of goodness and love, man shall let death have no sovereignty over his thoughts.*—And with this—I awake. For I have dreamed it out to the end, I have come to my goal.

Hans Castorp, his vision at least partially clarified, plunges again into the confused life of the flat-land, where gigantic wars pass more and more into the hands of the man-gods Prometheus and Mohammed. . . . There are even more Castorps today. And through the shadow of the Terror there falls before seeking eyes the shadow of Maitreya. Man is not satisfied with contemporary man, and he projects in the very moment of his agony the image of what he wishes to be. In the falling of an age a new age seeks to make its way. The form is unclear and the future uncertain—but a new man-god seeks birth. Men are working to carve the image of the new man toward whom they grope.

Maitreyism may supply the answer to contemporary man's search for a rallying ground on which to consolidate his forces and from which to invade the future. Nietzsche's question, Who is to become master of the earth? has grown ever more insistent. Men are now being forced to think and feel and act in planetary terms; the earth is no longer an aggregate of autonomous regions each of which can go its independent way. What directive ideal is to chart the march into this planetary future? Where is the vision great enough, clear enough, dynamic enough to meet the challenge which earth-leadership imposes?

It has been the contention of these pages that the crucial issue is the choice as to the ideal of man to whom allegiance shall be given. For such choice will determine a hierarchy of values under the supreme personality value which it accepts; will make for itself a preferred morality, art, religion; will create for itself a society, since in the last analysis men can only approve or disapprove of social institutions in terms of the men and women they produce.

Such a choice is neither fated nor arbitrary. The personality of an individual is greatly influenced by his biological constitution, but not uniquely determined by it; the society in which he lives helps to influence the ideal to which he gives allegiance, and his own reflection may be one determining factor. The choice is not a mechanical resultant of biological and social factors, nor is it arbitrary in the sense that it can be made without being influenced by these factors. Nothing in a description of the types of personality which have obtained and do obtain makes it inevitable that these types shall always persist or persist in any fixed numerical ratio: it is perfectly possible by breeding and training to control the types and their relative predominance. Mankind is not committed to a bare acceptance of one or another of the patterns of personality which history exemplifies. Even where the larger outlines of a type remain recognizable, differences come in with every change of cultural conditions, and with every act of reflection. The Buddhist will not be exactly the same in an occidental or an oriental environment, nor exactly the same in two historic epochs of either culture; a person who thinks out the consequences of following any way of life will change to some degree the way of life he set out to follow. No "determinism of types of personality" is to be substituted for an "economic determinism" or a determinism of any other kind. There is no "inevitability" in choosing the Maitreyan as an ideal for oneself or for the preferred type of the human community.

Yet we have given some of the grounds which free this choice from arbitrariness. We have seen the concessions which certain of the historic religions make to the Maitreyan ideal within their professed acceptance of some other path of life; we have noted the biological and psychological facts which seem to show the difficulties and dangers which arise when any one segment of the organism and any one set of temperamental characteristics is given a too privileged place; we have tried to show the presence in Western culture of conflicting traits which seem to indicate Maitreyism as a possible goal for this culture; we have argued that this attitude combines the attitudes of the Orient and the Occident—as any attitude must do that is to be adequate to a planetary epoch; we have suggested to each type of person that a Maitreyan society would give to him the most favorable environment for his development compatible with the development of other persons. Beyond this it is not possible to go; each individual must take by himself the next step. *The way there is none.*

The person who finds the figure of Maitreya expressive of himself, or of the self he chooses to be, or at least of the preferred type in whose hands he wishes to see the instruments of social control, has as his first duty and privilege the task of living—wherever he be—in the light of his ideal. Whether he be thinker, or artist, or statesman, or churchman, or employer, or laborer, or student, or teacher, his activities are needed if the ideal is to assume the stamp of actuality. His ideal should give him the release, the courage, the incentive for the arduous labors and the unique joy to which the ideal is a lure.

Where, if anywhere, shall the Maitreyan ideal find social habitation? I should like to believe that the United States will assume this historic task. Certain it is that this hope is not fantastic, even if it be mistaken. There is deep frustration here, much uncertainty, blocked energies, superficiality piled high, aimless objectivity, hidden fears, wide disillusionment. The Promethean will falters; the Apollonians who seek for control have become frantic; the Mohammedans peep in at the window. If possessiveness is, as Thomas Wolfe insisted, the root evil which blocks a creative future, it is also true that this evil has deep roots—and the drastic social changes which are necessary will meet strong resistance. And yet—this is not the whole story. Powerful energies seek liberation, there is respect both for individual differences and for the common needs which must be commonly met, sufficient chaos and flexibility exist to break the forming mold, the sciences and the arts move with expectant vitality, there is a tradition of religious tolerance, imperfectly functioning political forms yet permit of pervasive changes in the social structure. The old symbols are not adequate to express or to direct what is in fact taking place. Perhaps the attitude of Maitreyism can unlock this frustration, conquer this fear, direct this energy? Perhaps this is yet to be what we have so proudly claimed, a New World, and not the last grave of the dying West? Perhaps the shadow of Maitreya which we now discern is but omen for the sound of his feet on these shores as he strides to encircle the earth?

Whatever be the course of the immediate or the remote future, the Maitreyan's task is clear. His hope as to the future is grounded in his view of human nature and his outlook on human history. He feels that he is the inheritor of the deepest traditions of the Orient and the Occident, merging the buddhistic and dionysian traditions of the former with the Christianized promethean spirit of the latter. He recognizes that none of the special religions is any longer able to be the sole vehicle for the image of the new man which is forming. He believes that this new image will be embodied in a new religious spirit which will supplement, though not necessarily for all persons supplant, the existing religions. He thinks it important to fix this image of Maitreyan man and form the attitude of generalized detached-attachment, for this image and attitude give direction into the future—and only an image and attitude give such direction. Ancient prediction believed that five thousand years would elapse between the death of Gautama Buddha and the birth of Maitreya, the next Enlightened One. Ancient mythology taught that a Buddha went through many reincarnations in the course of his development preceding his birth. For the Maitreyan these predictions and legends need not be given more than a symbolic character: ideals take time to work themselves out and the efforts of many lives are needed that they may take on the stamp of actuality.

Life is lived in the present, and the future issues only out of a present. One lives now in the light of ideals held for the future, otherwise future and present alike are betrayed. The Maitreyan believes with the former Buddha that salvation is a state of living, to be obtained in this life by one's own efforts; he replaces the vague and misleading doctrine of the extinction of desire by the generalized doctrine of detached-attachment, and he extends this attitude to the whole self, to other selves, to the whole cosmos—and to the attitude of detached-attachment itself. To feel oneself the carrier of oriental and occidental heritages into a new future; to link one's muscles to the material for one's will; to banish the clouds from the mind; to cherish diversity; to merge with awed delight in the great universe-play; to relinquish the possessive grip on the self, and on other selves, and on all things; to stand before the self, and other selves and other things with the alertness, the receptivity, the warmth, the challenge of a friend: this defines the Maitreyan's nirvana, attained here, in this life, now,—whatever be his future or man's future or the future sport of the ample universe.

Index and Acknowledgments

Acknowledgments

I AM indebted to Professor Walter E. Clark for conversations on Buddhism; Professor A. Eustace Haydon was kind enough to read the book in manuscript; the assistance of Ruth Herschberger in the preparation of this work has been so extensive that I regard her as a collaborator in its production.

Permission to reprint passages from the following books has been given by author, editor, and publisher:

Thomas Aquinas: Selected Writings, edited by M. C. D'Arcy, in Everyman's Library (E. P. Dutton and Co., New York City; J. M. Dent and Sons, London); *The Bhagavad Gita,* translated by Annie Besant (The Theosophical Publishing House, Madras, India); *The Tao Teh Ching,* translated by Ch'a Ta-Kao (Buddhist Lodge, London); *A Common Faith,* John Dewey (Yale University Press); *Liberalism and Social Action,* John Dewey (G. P. Putnam's Sons); *A Buddhist Bible,* edited by Dwight Goddard (Thetford, Vermont); *The Selected Poetry of Robinson Jeffers* (Random House, Inc.); *The Magic Mountain,* Thomas Mann (Alfred A. Knopf); *The Works of Friedrich Nietzsche,* edited by Dr. Oscar Levy (The Macmillan Company, New York City; George Allen and Unwin, London); *Goethe's Faust,* translated by George M. Priest (Alfred A. Knopf); *Letters to a Young Poet,* Rainer Maria Rilke, translated by M. D. Herter Norton (W. W. Norton and Company); *A Season in Hell,* Arthur Rimbaud, translated by Delmore Schwartz (New Directions); *The Varieties of Human Physique,* W. H. Sheldon (Harper & Brothers); *The Life of Buddha,* Edward J. Thomas (Alfred A. Knopf, New York City; Kegan Paul, Trench, Trubner and Company, London).

CATHOLIC THEOLOGICAL UNION
BL80.2.M671973   C001
PATHS OF LIFE CHICAGO

3 0311 00006 7194

BL 80.2 .M67 1973

Morris, Charles W.
  1903-1979.

Paths of life